Four Open Field Books

Jan Willem Kaiser

Four Open Field Books

New Inspiration in Judaeo-Christian Spirituality

With an introduction by
Rogier Fentener van Vlissingen

JWK Publications

Published by:
JWK Publications
a division of Millennium Management Incorporated
40 Rampart Road
South Norwalk, CT 06854-2417

Translated by: Rogier Fentener van Vlissingen

¹⁰/₉₄

First edition in one volume.
The individual monographs in this volume were previously published in a limited, numbered first edition between 1987 and 1989.

This book was produced using Ventura Publisher, and typeset in Century Schoolbook, Book Antiqua, Bookman Old Style, and formatted with PSPublisher. The manuscript was output to film on a Linotronic 330 typesetter. Manufactured in the United States of America by BookCrafters of Chelsea, Mi. Printed on 60# Booktext Natural, acid free paper.

ISBN 0-943185-03-3
Library of Congress Catalog Card Number 92-074647

Ventura Publisher is a registered trademark of Ventura Software Inc.
Century Schoolbook, Book Antiqua, and Bookman Old Style, are trademarks of Monotype Typographic Inc.
PS Publisher is a trademark of The Graphics Art Division.
Linotronic 330 is a registered trademark of Linotype-Hell Company
Booktext Natural is a trademark of BookCrafters

Acknowledgement

This book could not have been realized without the loving support of my wife Nancy, who labored endlessly on the proofreading of this often very difficult material. Many others have contributed as well, and I will not even attempt to present an exhaustive list, but offer a general thanks from this place. Special thanks must go to the foundation that manages Kaiser's literary estate, the Stichting Open Veld Werk in Holland. Their support made this publication possible.

Table of Contents

Jan Willem Kaiser: An introduction to his life and work, and his place in the Judaeo-Christian spiritual tradition

by Rogier Fentener van Vlissingen

Four Open Field Books is a collection of short monographs by the Dutch author Jan Willem Kaiser. They make an ideal introduction to his work. They show the enormous range of his insight, yet they are concise and complete in themselves. We hope to publish translations of the author's other works in due course.

This introduction serves three purposes. First, it gives relevant details about the author's life, to provide some sense of how the author lived the truths that he spoke, and wrote about. Some of the author's sources are discussed, which will aid in understanding some details that might be unclear without such background information. Second, a summary of the material in this volume is followed by a description of the author's other works, so it can be appreciated in the appropriate context. Third and last, an overview of his principal teachings is used as the basis of an analysis of the author's place in Western Spiritual tradition. Inevitably, this third aspect in particular is less factual in nature, and strongly reflects the personal experience of the writer of this introduction.

Even though these four books were published a generation ago, their true relevance in some ways was never clearer than today. We are rediscovering spirituality, and getting away from the traditional theology of Judaism and Christianity. The Bible remains a source of inspiration, in which we may gradually come to discover new spiritual meaning. Kaiser's work opens the door for such a rediscovery. For one thing he included what apocryphal material was available in his studies, as well as the rich material of myth and legend from the East and the West. He consistently uncovers the spiritual significance in long-familiar material, and shows us the rich guidance for our life's spiritual journey that is available in the Western tradition. The inner meaning of much of this material was lost to the extent that we lived with church traditions which emphasized an external God, and the mediation of institutions and ritual between man and God. Kaiser brings us back to the direct personal relevance of Jesus, as the one who shows us, and who is the Way, the Truth and the Life.

In a number of ways J.W.Kaiser's work seems to foreshadow the teachings that were to appear fifteen years after his death in the form of A Course In Miracles. Kaiser developed his material by a close examination of the traditional literary sources, including a lot of scholarly work on the translation of Biblical material. Along these lines, he developed a very explicit and clear understanding of spiritual development in the Judaeo-Christian tradition. He included in his work some material that was channeled from Jesus, via two people with whom he was in contact, but this was a relatively small amount of material. A Course In Miracles, which was channeled from Jesus in its entirety, offers a new look at several Biblical passages and concepts, sometimes as a total restatement, sometimes in the form of a new reading. The parallels between this material and Kaiser's work are often striking. What Kaiser culled out of traditional sources with great effort, the Course offers in the form of a radical restatement. We will look into this in more detail below.

The central issue is the understanding of the journey of salvation as a path that is open to all of us. Its nature reflects the reality we experience, and thus of the very structure of our awareness. In the present collection it is perhaps *The Open Field and the Field of Good and Evil*, which offers the most comprehensive vision of our reality, and the nature of the path of salvation. It is a seminal work on spiritual cosmogony and cosmology in the Judaeo-Christian tradition.

His Life's work

J an Willem Kaiser was born in Hoorn, Holland, February 27, 1897. He was the son of a doctor. As a boy he also wanted to become a doctor, but he saw his dreams thwarted by his father's early death. He had to abandon his studies to start supporting himself and his family. He worked in the insurance industry, until the time he felt guided to resign his post to pursue his writing and speaking full time, in 1946. Later in his life he realized that his life's work was indeed heavily focused on healing, but in quite a different way than he had dreamt of as a boy.

Aside from pursuing a career in the business world, Kaiser was an avid student of Hebrew, Greek, and Aramaic, and of many spiritual traditions, including astrology and Kabbalah. As early as 1929 he published an article on the meaning of classical drama as a reflection of spiritual experience in our life. But his major literary inheritance to which the *Four Open Field Books* are an introduction, stems from the period after

1946, when he felt guided to cull *the Word* out from among the clutter, and present it to the modern seeker in a way that was newly accessible, and immediately relevant. The emphasis of his work was on undertaking the spiritual journey in this life, rather than on speculation and theory. He shows us the immediacy of experience behind many traditions, and its practical relevance in our life today.

His most important work is his new translation and esoteric interpretation of the Gospel according to Mark. His further work, beyond the four monographs presented here, consists of essays on a wide range of spiritual topics, many of which have been published in book form. His writing style is stern, archaic, and sometimes arcane, especially when he incorporates channeled material and expressions which are not common to everyday language. His choice of words is a cross between the King James Version and Shakespeare, and he sometimes takes poetic license in employing very awkward sentence structures for effect. He can come on strong, with a sternness that has overtones of a fundamentalist preacher, yet it is evident throughout that he wrote from a pure love. He labored hard to get things on paper to truly reflect the inspiration from which he worked; his deep love and uncompromising dedication are tangible. Patience on the part of the reader is a definite virtue! The translations in this volume have sought to remain faithful to the original, and the appearance of stilted language is hopefully not a sign of a bad translation, but a conscious attempt to be true to the Dutch text.

In the course of his searching Kaiser became acquainted with Theosophy, Krishnamurti, Anthroposophy, Rosicrucianism, Christian Science, the Oxford movement, Yoga, Judaism, Christianity, Buddhism, Hinduism, Islam, Psychology, the Holy Grail, Near Eastern Religions, and Astrology, and undoubtedly I forgot a few. His studies of these sources were quite thorough. What is clear in his work, is that through his own authentic spiritual experience he did see through all these varied traditions to the eternal nature of the spiritual reality and experience of man. In his work the expressions of all of these traditions are clarified and made understandable as guidance on our journey back to God.

In 1946 he experienced guidance to dedicate himself wholly to his speaking and writing work. The mission he accepted as his, was in close conjunction with Ms. Margaretha Hofmans. Ms. Hofmans had a very specific role in their cooperation, which was very distinct from Kaiser's. Ms. Hofmans' inspiration was to listen to people's problems and facilitate their healing by offering them inspiration to accept the loving presence of God's Help (Jesus) in their lives. Often this would involve specific channeled answers to issues that people brought to her. It would appear that within the context of their cooperation, hers was the one on one work with people, whereas his was the writing, and public speaking, and developing the conceptual aspects of their mission. It is relevant to know that any channeled words that appear in the text often were received by Ms. Hofmans. They are usually marked as: Logion. Some of these words were channeled by Mr. Frits Willem Bonk, another person who received channeled material, but who was not closely involved with their regular work.

Their cooperation also resulted in a long series of biannual conferences, starting in 1951, originally titled *Het Oude Loo,* after the castle where they were held, and later, from 1958 on, when they were held at a different location, named *The Open Field* - which in turn was a word play on the Dutch word "loo," which means a clearing in the forest, or an open field. The last of these meetings was held in 1968.

These meetings were an open forum for participants to discuss their spiritual journey, based on an introduction by a speaker. The text of an original invitation to these meetings has been included at the end of this volume. The meetings were attended by invitation only, but the format was totally non-denominational. Kaiser was a frequent speaker there. Some other speakers included Rabbi J. Soetendorp, Prof. Martin Buber, Dr. Erwin Zippert, William Aspden, Dr. Hans Müller Eckhard, Dr. Gustav Mensching, Oskar Köllerstroem, Norbert Löser, Linus Pauling, Prof. Dr. Graf Karlfried von Dürkheim, Gerald Bailey, Prof. Dr. Gilles Quispel, Prof. Dr. Annemarie Schimmel, Juan Mascaro, Joel S. Goldsmith, George Trevalyan, Christmas Humphreys, Dane Rhudhyar, and many others.

Perhaps the most important feature of Jan Willem Kaiser's work is that he makes us realize that everything but everything speaks to us of salvation. He helps us open our spiritual vision, and see the ultimate oneness in all religions and all traditions, not as a new Sufi-movement, a religion of all

16

religions, but as true enlightenment in which content, not form, guides us. And while he proves himself a careful and accomplished scholar in a number of places, he leaves no doubt that his only meaningful qualification for his writing and speaking was the experience of God's Love in his own life.

Jan Willem Kaiser died in 1960. Margaretha Hofmans died in 1968. Frits Willem Bonk died in 1987.

Four Open Field Books

The *Four Open Field Books* are mostly talks given at the Open Field convention, the only exception being *The Birth Pangs of New Man*, which was originally published as a book. The publication dates of these four little books cover a five year period towards the end of the author's life, and they represent an interesting summary of some major themes in his work.

Sanctification of Life is a talk that was given in 1955 at the Oude Loo Conference. The book speaks to us of accepting our life as a path to relinquish all our accustomed values, all the idols of the world of time and space. He describes how part of that journey is the experience of the presence of Jesus, God's Salvation, or God's Help, within us. Kaiser summarizes that path of transformation in which our ego, our temporal persona disintegrates and fades away in the following words: *Jesus, who we are not, and will not become, but Who appears in our place as 'we' no longer are, and let ourselves be demolished and transformed into what then can only be called **Jesus**.*

Religion and Religions is a talk originally given at the *Oude Loo* Convention on May 27th of 1956. The book starts from the recognition that the basic structure of the personality is that we build our own reality, in which we deny God. The main theme of the book is how we have the tendency to get lost in the variety of forms of religion, to the point of losing the original meaning of religion as service and dedication to God. The religions (plural) are all doctrines about God, and these doctrines become our idols which we worship in lieu of accepting our own direct relationship with God. The book then points the way back to that relationship.

The Open Field and the Field of Good and Evil is a talk that was given at the *Open Field Conventions* on August 28-30, 1959 at Zeist, Holland. The talk was originally given in

English, but the present edition is mostly a new translation from the book that was published in Dutch on the basis of that same talk. The book version was clearer than the speech, so this translation was guided mostly by it. The book focuses on the meaning of astrological symbolism, and helps us see the world in psychological, and spiritual terms. Of particular importance are the clues to the astrological symbolism of the Bible provided in this book. It brings unprecedented clarity to this area, which has been the subject of much muddled speculation and obfuscation.

The Open Field and the Field of Good and Evil contrasts two modes of living, which Kaiser calls respectively the action of the Cross, and the way of the Cross. In terms of A Course In Miracles, the action of the Cross would equate to living under the guidance of the ego, and thus crucifixion, whereas the way of the Cross would be living under the guidance of the Holy Spirit, and thus accepting every life situation as a classroom, and a further step on the Atonement path. In his discussion of the symbolism of the Zodiac, he contrasts these two modes of response as they relate to the astrological signs. The action of the Cross represents living under the will of the separated (false) self, and the way of the Cross would represent living God's Will. The ego inevitably experiences the latter choice as a sacrifice (crucifixion), but in reality it is the sacrifice of nothing (an illusion), as A Course In Miracles reminds us in many places.

Choosing for the separation, we doom ourselves to repeat the same patterns "forever," while, when choosing to experience the zodiac with Jesus, we undo the error. As Kaiser put it: "For all the Twelve Gates, *as long as we pass through them in reverse direction,* give access to the Holy Jerusalem."

There are few, if any, books in our Western spiritual tradition which summarize in so powerful a way as this little monograph does, the nature of our reality, and practical implications of the journey of salvation. The integration of astrological and biblical symbolism leads to an integrated understanding of the nature of our mind in the traditon of traditional psychology. In a way this book summarizes the concepts that underlie the author's major work on the Gospel of Mark.

Birth Pangs of New Man was first published in 1958. The theme of this book is an evolutionary understanding of our journey back home. This book, like *Religion and Religions* departs from a description of the unreality of our world. The main theme of the book is to look at the world with different eyes, and to learn to study "the book of nature" as a reminder. After identifying how and why traditional Christianity is an ego-religion, based in fact on the denial of God, the author teaches us to recognize God's plan for Salvation everywhere we look. It shows how in the end we are doomed to fail in our denial of the truth, and thus are bound to commence the journey home, in following Jesus, as the Way, the Truth, and the Life.

The book also expresses the author's views on an evolutionary change towards greater spiritual awareness in the world at large, as a long term trend.

Other works

The Wisdom of Fairy Tales, 1946. This book is a most remarkable spiritual analysis of several popular fairy tales and myths.

The Mysteries of Jesus in our Lives, 2nd Edition 1952. This book is a series of essays around the experience of Jesus in our lives. Drawing on all spiritual traditions, it dismisses the clutter, and focuses the reader on the essence behind all the variations in form. Sections deal with the symbolism of many Biblical books and themes, as well as the apocryphal acts of the apostles. Other contributions are on astrology, the chakras, and an extensive esoteric vocabulary which gives etymological explanations of terms from many traditions in the mold of classical Jewish commentaries, combining form and content to express the spiritual significance of terms.

Experience of the Gospel, 1950. This book is an new translation of and an esoteric commentary to the gospel of Mark. It refocuses the Gospel from a historical treatise, as the churches have traditionally treated it, to a living experience. The book discovers many aspects of sloppy translation which have found their way into the "received" Bible translation, and which uniformly have disguised the spiritual meaning of the text, and have facilitated the theological misrepresentations on which organized religions built their systems. Specifically, the book shows in great detail the underlying nature of Jesus' presence in our lives, namely A Time, Times, and a half a Time, or three and one half complete passes through the Zodiac, during which period our mortal structure (lower self) is broken down, to make room for the manifestation of Jesus. There are few if any books that demonstrate in so much detail how the Gospel models the spiritual journey for us, and represents guidance for all time.

Zodiacal symbolism of the Gospel according to Mark. (1959) This publication is an adjunct to the previous one, and it contains a diagram that analyzes the astrological structure of the Gospel according to Mark.

Ascension to Life. This is a collection of three long essays, based on presentations held in the years 1959 and 1960 in Amsterdam. The first one deals with the spiritual symbolism of bread, the bread of Life, as spiritual nourishment that sustains us in our journey through the desert. The second one treats the symbolism of the solstice, interpreting it as a parable for the soul's turning back to its source, God. The last essay deals with the meaning of ascension, as the path of salvation. These essays are in many ways the culmination of Kaiser's work. They integrate an incredible wealth of material on their respective topics, and they seem more concentrated than anything else he wrote.

Gnostic tradition

By implication, Jan Willem Kaiser stands in the Gnostic tradition - though he nowhere labels himself as such. But I believe it is relevant to think of him in those terms, in order to understand his relationship to Western spirituality.

The reasons he stands in the Gnostic tradition, are many. Most obvious are his frequent identification of our reality as a delusion, a pseudo-reality as he would have called it. In the early pages of the *Birth Pangs of New Man* this theme is developed. In the first few pages of *Religion and Religions,* the author brings it up again. Those are just two obvious places. Throughout his work he develops the notion of how we are caught up in our temporal awareness, while our calling is to wake up to our eternal reality. He never develops a position quite so explicit as some of the Gnostics, and as A Course In Miracles would later do in separating God from the creator god, (Ialdabaoth, the demiurge, the ego), but he does explicitly identify man's projections onto God of his own separation thought, as in: *The Almighty does not 'drive man out' from this Heart of Creation (Paradise, Ed.), but man abandons this Heart and seeks to justify himself by projecting his motive and the consequence of it as a punishment or curse by God.* (in: *The Open Field and the Field of Good and Evil*, p.84)

Given the many references in his work to the pseudo reality in which we live, and our misguided "valuation of matter" where he clearly implies that the world of our senses is not reality, it seems almost contradictory that he continues in the traditional position that God created the world, and similarly that God acts in the world. In many places it is clear however that he speaks of an inner God, and not of an external God. This is especially recognizable in what he says about the meaning of the Sonship and the fulfilling of our relationship to the Father. The later view of A Course In Miracles, namely that the very physical reality of the world is a creation of the ego, and not of God, would resolve this contradiction by totally abandoning the dualism that grants the world any objective reality at all.

Kaiser understands *the Gospel* as a psychological and spiritual process that is relevant to our life today - focusing entirely on the inner experience of God. He views *the Gospels* (the books) as the imperfect expressions of people who describe for their readership their awareness of the coming of Jesus into their life. Especially in his translation of and commentary to the symbolism of the Gospel according to Mark, it is very clear that he takes no interest in the historical events. What he seeks to demonstrate is how the Gospel is the expression of an inner process. Throughout this work it is very clear that he is not speaking about a world out there, but about a world in here. He is speaking of the process of salvation as a process in the mind, and moreover a process that is accessible to anyone who responds to the calling of the Voice of God. This puts him firmly in the mystical tradition. It also is inherently a Gnostic position, in that it teaches the direct following of Jesus, without the aid of any intermediaries - which is one of the points on which the Church rejected the Gnostics. To him, Jesus is the one who shows us the way, and our path is to follow him, and accept him as our teacher - Kaiser does not make him special, as the churches have, because that notion gives us an excuse not to follow him.

In his volume of essays, *The Mysteries of Jesus in our Lives,* he explicitly embraces the apocryphal (and very Gnostic) acts of the apostles as part and parcel of the tradition about Jesus, without in any way depicting them as inferior to the canonical traditions. Finally, he strongly expresses the view that beginning with Paul, the tradition of Jesus was perverted into a worldly doctrine, a moral code. Thus he radically throws out traditional Christian theology, and seeks to bring us back to an understanding of the original message of Jesus. Throughout his work, the emphasis is on the fulfillment of the Son-Father relationship between ourselves and God, as the true essence of our life.

A note on astrological symbolism

Some clarification on Kaiser's use of astrological symbolism is in order. In terms of the zodiac itself, he finds great significance in the Greek mythological tradition[1] which emphasizes that the zodiac at one level falls into two halves. In this tradition it was thought that there is a division that runs between Cancer and Leo on one side, and Capricorn and Aquarius on the other. Traditionally it was thought that the soul incarnated (descended on earth) in Cancer (really on the transition between Leo and Cancer), and rose up to heaven in Capricorn (more precisely in the transition from Capricorn to Aquarius).

The basic structure of the zodiac reflected an earthly half, and a heavenly half, traditionally called day and night halves. Using another analogy, they are the Sun half (the Aquarius through Leo segment) and the Moon half (the Cancer through Capricorn segment). In line with this tradition, it is obvious that the planets past Saturn belong with the signs Aquarius through Aries, as they denote more spiritual qualities.

Accordingly, this school of astrological thinking treats Pluto as the ruler of Aries, not the ruler of Scorpio as is presently assumed by many popular authors, especially in the U.S.A. The principal proponent of this school of astrology was Th.J.J.

---

[1] For an excellent source on classical mythology, the reader may wish to refer to: Robert Graves, The Greek Myths, Penguin Books.

Ram, whose book on psychological astrology is still one of the best ever written in any language. This tradition still lives on today, with a number of astrologers in Holland, England, and Germany, and a few in the U.S.A.

Further, this school of astrology also surmised the existence of three hypothetical planets, which would round out the system: Persephone, Hermes, and Demeter which would successively replace the night rulerships of Venus in Taurus, Mercury in Gemini, and the Moon in Cancer.

Finally, he makes reference to the mythological notion of the Garden of Eden as the Center (Unity, Origin, Heaven), in which grew both the Tree of Life, and the Tree of the Knowledge of Good and Evil. The fundamental division of the zodiac in two halves is the one referred to above, which has been reflected in traditional art as a tree. There are various traditions that equate the zodiac to a tree in similar fashion. There are not a great deal of useful sources for this material in the English language. The interested reader is referred to a brilliant German book, Julius Schwabe's, *Archetyp und Tierkreis*, Benno Schwabe & Co, Basel, 1951, which is an exhaustive treatment of the world's mythological traditions and their relationship to astrology, approached from a Jungian perspective.

Astrological references are everywhere in Kaiser's work, and since he implicitly assumes some familiarity on the part of the readership with these concepts, and in particular with the school of Th.J.J. Ram, the reader is encouraged to refer to this section when necessary. In general however, Kaiser is a minimalist astrologer, and he does not encourage studying astrology, but he advocates developing one's natural intuition about astrological contexts in one's life.

The Bible

The Judaeo-Christian tradition is central to Kaiser's work. He liberally includes other traditions, but fundamentally he stands in the Biblical tradition, because it is the dominant factor in the Western world. At the same time, he completely restates "accepted" Christian positions, and thereby distances himself from what most avowed Christians would believe.

His source is primarily his own inspiration, or guidance. His material is the Bible, always including the apocryphal traditions, to the extent that they were available at the time. He shows us the spiritual foundation of the Biblical tradtion. In style, he frequently follows the model of traditional Jewish exegesis, analyzing the meaning of all Biblical names for clues to the significance of important Bible stories. In content, he is led primarily by his own penetrating inspiration, and never biased by "accepted" interpretations.

Where the New Testament is concerned, he points out a number of mistranslations in places where the original Greek text preserved a spiritual meaning, which was not understood by later translators, and thus distorted. He makes the interesting point that the Vulgate, the first Latin translation of the Bible, by St. Jerome, frequently preserves these spiritual meanings of words, where later translations totally obfuscate these meanings.

Examples of this approach include the Greek word *epiousios*, before bread, in the Lord's prayer. This difficult adjective is translated in the Vulgate as *super substantial* (Latin: panis supersubstantialis), indicating clearly that spiritual nourishment is the meaning. Most, if not all later translations distort the word into meaning *daily*, which is a tenuous derivation at best. Most importantly, the practice of translating the original expression as *daily bread*, gave rise to the widespread misunderstanding that God is somehow in competition with your local baker. Certainly such a translation represents a total loss of the original meaning of the phrase.

Another important example is the translation of the word *monogenes* before son in the New Testament. An honest appraisal of the Greek etymology would lead one to read this word as one-born, born-as-one. Again, St. Jerome leaves this reading intact by (mostly) translating the word as *unigenitus*. Later translators did not understand the spiritual significance of the oneness of the Son of God (Christ, the Sonship), and reinterpreted the word in the sense of viewing the person Jesus as God's **only** son. Doing so is generally disastrous from the standpoint of the spiritual significance of the expression, and in practice it led to the singling out of Jesus as somehow special (divine) including on a more mundane level the confusing position in popular Catholic tradition that the historical person Jesus did not have any brothers or sisters, even though there is reference to this fact in the Gospels.

Kaiser points out that the emphasis of Paulist theology on Jesus' dying for our sins is an utter misunderstanding of the meaning of the Gospels. E.g. in *The Open Field* he says: *'dying on the cross' means to be 'lifted up' beyond the restrictions of our cranium*[2], *which is the product of our 'fallen' state and therefore can never be liberating, but will ever more 'bind' us to that consciousness of ours which splits everything into contrasting halves.*

The author similarly rectifies our understanding of the betrayal of Jesus by Judas. Also here he pursues the point based as much on his own understanding and inspiration as on exegesis of the Greek text of the New Testament. The pivotal insight is that the objective meaning of the Greek word that describes Judas' "betrayal," is not betrayal, but a very neutral, non-accusatory "handing over." Perhaps the most elaborate treatment of the meaning of Judas is found in *Birth Pangs of New Man*. There he explains how Judas represents the fear of the spirit in all of us, and how in our confusion, we seek to grasp it, and put it in a box, and thus kill the form. But, the content is not the form, and as the author points out, by this time the first steps on the path of Salvation have been taken. In *The Open Field and the Field of Good and Evil*, the meaning of Judas is discussed further under Capricorn, since Judas is the Capricorn disciple.

Another important point is the translation in Mk 15:34 of the Aramaic *Eloi, Eloi lama sabachtani?* Kaiser emphasizes that the proper translation of the word *lama* should be *what for*, rather than the common translation with *why*. The difference between the two is in the fact that *why* asks for cause and thus evokes guilt - an ego concept - whereas *what for* presumes a total faith in God's plan of the Atonement which we merely do not understand in our separated consciousness.

In *The Mysteries of Jesus in our Lives*, Kaiser reinterprets many Old Testament stories in a spiritual light. Guided by his insights, we can learn to newly understand many familiar stories as pure spiritual guidance of the highest order. Most

---

[2] Editor's note: The word Golgotha means cranium.

of traditional Paulist as well as Jewish theology is rejected, although he implicitly pays homage to traditional commentaries (Rashi, Talmud, Midrashim and Kabbalah) where they amplify his interpretations, even if he seldom cites them explicitly.

A Course In Miracles

In many areas it seemed as if the teachings of A Course In Miracles were foreshadowed in the work of J.W.Kaiser. My own experience has been that after twenty-five years of studying Kaiser's work and one year of studying the Course, I find myself having an easier time understanding Jan Willem Kaiser. Most importantly, the strict non-dualism of the Course resolves some internal contradictions which seem to remain in Kaiser's speaking of God as the founder of the world. Kaiser's work however covers many areas that are never discussed in the Course - on the inner meaning of Biblical tradition - and perhaps most importantly he shows how the message of salvation was always there, ready for anyone who wished to follow it.

In a general sense a major issue that runs through Kaiser's work is to show up in detail how what we made of the world is a travesty of our heritage as children of God, and very much a defense against the acceptance of our part in the sonship, and our relationship to the Father. In this respect he clearly addresses issues in a manner that foreshadow the Course. On another level, he speaks very much in terms of God's acting in our life, and in the world, and of a spiritual significance of evolutionary processes in the world. He never clarifies this issue completely in terms of separating the levels of our dualistic world of experience in time and space, versus the non-dualistic unity of the Kingdom. He seems to brush past this important issue.

Kaiser can deepen our reading of the Bible beyond the traditions of accepted theology to a spiritual level of understanding that makes it newly relevant. He salvages the message of the Bible through his "spiritual archaeology" on the material, thus rescuing the content from what the theologians have made of it. The Course on the other hand treats the Bible as an institution of Christian theology. In the Course Jesus proposes corrections directly, simply indicating that the Bible accounts were either not accurate or misunderstood. All this would seem to render the Bible obsolete, but that is hardly the point. In the end books don't matter, only experience does, as both Kaiser and the Course suggest. For now it is interesting to explore some of these points.

Religion and Religions could be an introduction to A Course In Miracles before its time. Kaiser's discussion of the separation ("the state of ficticitous isolations") in that book (p.70), could have come straight from the Course. And in *Birth Pangs of New Man*, among the present material the one book that would appear to have the least in common with the Course, he says: *The Way of Heaven evokes all wretchedness, everything that could be in the way of Peace; it calls all that had been artfully and carefully hidden and concealed into the foreground, so it shows itself and acts itself out, and thereby shows its lack of validity to itself* (p. 128). Here we could almost literally substitute the words "the process of A Course In Miracles," for the words "the Way of Heaven," and we would have a concise definition of what the Course is all about.

In *The Open Field and the Field of Good and Evil* (p. 110), he (re)defines the Last Judgement in terms that resonate with the Course, indicating that it is really our becoming aware of what is eternal (of God, Heavenly), and what is temporal. Likewise, on page 116, he defines the only decision (The One Thing Needful, the decision between Heaven and Hell) in terms that are strongly evokative of A Course In Miracles.

In terms virtually identical to the Course's language on special relationships, he describes our pursuit of horizontal relationships in lieu of the one vertical relationship (with God), which they are meant (by the ego) to replace. Similar to the Course he recognizes the value of such relationships as a classroom, and where Kaiser speaks of God's Holy Therapy, the Course speaks of Holy Relationships. He cautions against the typical ego reaction of rejecting the form - recognizing that type of action as merely the opposite of embracing it. For instance in his discussion of the path of the Buddha in *Sanctification of Life* he makes it very clear that acts of sacrificing our ties to the world are an ego-device and not manifestations of spiritual progress.

The Course emphasises the oneness of the Sonship, something which connects closely to the commentary Kaiser offers on the Son of God, born-as-one, as cited above. Interestingly

Ms. Hofmans in a newspaper interview expressed it as follows: *We are connected with each other at a deeper level than most of us think. A curious thing, that we all are part of one body.*[3] Although in choice of words this formulation may superficially differ from expressions we find in A Course In Miracles, in content she clearly speaks entirely the same language.

Another important parallel with the Course is Kaiser's emphasis on the fact that the concept of sin is not part of Jesus' message. He approaches this on the basis of the proper meaning of the Greek word *hamartia*, which is failure, failing, mistake, but not sin. In the last pages of *The Birth Pangs of New Man*, he points to the fact that Jesus' message concerns the "cancellation," the forgiveness of the failing, or the mistakes of the world. He makes the same point at several other places in his books.

The Course does not deal with the issue on the level of linguistics, but does say over and over again that the concept of sin is an ego concept, which serves to maintain the sway of guilt over us. As the Course puts it, to the Holy Spirit there are only mistakes, which can be corrected. From a historical point of view it is clear that the theological development of the concept of sin in the Paulist tradition is a reflection of how the world (the ego) distorted Jesus' message for its own unholy purposes. Kaiser points out in a footnote, that Luther in his Bible translation - which laid the foundation for the Protestant movement - attempted to undo this tradition of sin and guilt, by choosing a German word (*die Fehle*) which means error, mistake.

In several places Kaiser points out that the notion of Jesus' dying for our sins is a distortion of his message, and that this fundamental concept of so-called Christian theology, along with the deification of Jesus, was in fact an excuse for us *not* to have to follow him. The Course would later say that Jesus' crucifixion was merely an extreme example of the fact that God's love, not the world is our reality. A similar parallel is found in how both deal with the story of Judas, and our projection of guilt onto him, and though they treat this matter

[3] Interview in Elseviers Weekblad, Saturday, June 23, 1956.

28

in a superficially different manner, in essence they say the same thing. Judas is one of the Twelve, one of us, and entitled to forgiveness and love, for the "sin" we see in him is our sin.

The Course emphasizes heavily that we should wonder *what is it for,* rather than *why?* Kaiser points out the important difference between these two attitudes in the passage cited above in the Gospel of Mark. In general most all of the points raised above under the discussion of Kaiser's treatment of the Bible parallel closely what the Course offers on this topic.

On the whole the thoughts expressed in A Course In Miracles are different in form (specific usage etc.), but very similar in content to what Kaiser writes. Following what Kaiser has to say, we arrive at nearly all the same corrections to the accepted reading of the Bible as the Course offers. The question arises: How could Kaiser arrive at those same corrections, using merely the extant texts of the Old and New Testament (including Apocrypha)?

His approach is that the texts that were handed down to us have corrupted the message in several ways. Frequently the understanding of the authors was faulty, or partial at best, and their expression was therefore clumsy and sometimes misleading. Further corruption then happened in subsequent translations, where increasingly (Paulist) theological misinterpretation took over from the original intent of the text. Thus we have layer upon layer of corruption. His attempt to uncover the true meaning of these traditions invariably involves both careful critical scholarship and dedicated listening to our deepest intuition as we progress on our own journey of salvation.

A detailed reconciliation between Kaiser's work and A Course In Miracles would serve no purpose, but their convergence on several issues is noteworthy. The Course appears to us in the English language, and addresses The Bible as such: a translated document, infused as it is with the ego-bound theology that has dominated the Christian churches. The Course then offers its corrections. Kaiser treats the Bible not as the literal word of God, but as the imperfect expressions of imperfect people who struggled to express their own experience on the journey to salvation. By going back to the original text he recovers a lot of spiritual meaning that was lost to us in later translations and theological interpretations. Thus on one level, when the Course speaks of the Bible it means what limited human scribes and Christian theology made of the Bible, and specifically of Jesus' message. Kaiser, on the other hand, sets out to uncover the real message from underneath that corrupted tradition. For all their differences in form, the outcomes, the specific corrections to our understanding of our tradition show remarkable convergence.

It appears tempting to students of the Course to accept the Course's corrections to the Bible, and to throw out the Bible with the bath water. Kaiser's work suggests that it may be rewarding to read past the imperfections and rediscover the Bible as speaking to us of the same eternal spiritual realities which we will now increasingly learn to recognize everywhere in our lives. We can understand the many instances in the Bible where ego projections onto God get in the way, and paint a picture of the ego's version of god (the Demiurge) instead of the true God. If we are inclined to follow the linguistic research that Jan Willem Kaiser undertook, we would find that a careful reading of the original texts suggest an entirely different meaning than our de-spiritualized translations do in several places. Or, we can simply accept his observations in this area and follow his commentary - it will help us see these traditional writings in quite a new light.

A clear correspondence in content of A Course In Miracles and J. W. Kaiser is in identifying precisely what gets us started on the path to salvation. Kaiser speaks of John-Consciousness, after John the Baptist, and he indicates that the beginning of the path is to become aware that everything that happens in our life is a God Given Opportunity, so we become available to learn the lessons that are there. This is based on the etymology of the name John (Jehochanan), which means God Gives Graciously. The Course teaching says that when we turn to the Holy Spirit instead of the ego, everything we encounter becomes a classroom for the Atonement, rather than the prison that the ego makes it. The completion of the process Kaiser calls Jesus-Consiousness, and the Course calls living in the real world, or, with a Biblical reference, being in this world, but not of it, which Jesus exemplified for us. Both emphasize that the first prerequisite for any spiritual progress is to suspend our judgment, for by judging we drag the past into the present, and prevent ourselves from experiencing the holy significance of the now.

Perhaps it is most specifically in *The Open Field and the Field of Good and Evil* that Kaiser presents a model of reality that comes close to the Course's view. Early in the book he argues that God does not drive man out of Paradise (Heaven), man chooses to abandon it. Towards the end of the book, he makes it clear that man must "give up his life to accept it anew," and that "man has the power to do this out of his own free will, and there is nothing for which God loves man as much as for this deed of love." Taken together, this sounds very similar to the Course's view of how the trouble started (a bad dream), and the "little willingness" that is asked of us to begin our way home.

Careful reflection on the nature of reality, and the nature of the mind as presented in this monograph, imply a concept very close to the holographic model of reality that underlies the Course.

CONCLUSION

An important difference between the work of Jan Willem Kaiser, and A Course In Miracles is in the detailed metaphysics and psychology that the Course offers. Kaiser speaks of our pseudo-reality, and recognizes how projection of our own unhappiness makes us see enemies in the world (beginning with the angry God of the Old Testament), but nowhere does he offer the extensive spiritual and psychological framework that is the hallmark of A Course In Miracles. The metaphysics of the Course constitute an end-run past the ego, to make us immediately recognize at least to some degree what our divine birthright is. From that point of view giving up the ego is no big deal. In J. W. Kaiser's work we do find more of an emphasis on the pain of giving up, and we find that he speaks to us more in our personal awareness, where we certainly do experience pain and loss associated with losing the uneasy comfort of the long familiar conceptual framework of our ego-world.

Equally significant is the fact that Kaiser appears to retain the dualistic position that is typical of most of Judaeo-Christian thought. Even though he expresses that we mostly live in a pseudo-reality that is made up of our projections, he nevertheless seems to ascribe some tangible reality to the physical universe, and more importantly to conceive of God as acting in the world. In this area the strict non-dualistic position of A Course In Miracles certainly is clearer. It may also be easier to accept these days, as the implications of quantum mechanics are starting to become familiar, and a holographic model of reality is beginning to become acceptable.

It should be noted that, within the holographic concept of reality that A Course In Miracles proposes, the process of our waking up to reality could logically be experienced by the personality as an experience of Jesus, the Holy Spirit, or angels, within our life. Or, in Kaiser's own words, reflecting the same "transform" from holographic to linear, *In every one so confronted, paying attention and conceiving expectations works as 'being spoken to' and 'being promised things.'* (*The Open Field and the Field of Good and Evil*, p. 84) The apparent contradictions may therefore not be as significant as they seem at first.

One important contribution that the work of Jan Willem Kaiser has to make for our day, is to separate the Bible from Paulist theology. The Bible is not the problem, but the theological (and psychological!) interpretations given to it are. As I write this, I am a student of A Course In Miracles, and I have no doubt that through that book Jesus speaks to me, the same Jesus, the presence of God's Love in my life, which was pointed out to me earlier in my life by the work of Jan Willem Kaiser, Ms. Hofmans, and F.W. Bonk. Kaiser's work opens the door on an understanding of the spiritual meaning of the Biblical tradition. The depth and detail of guidance concerning the process of salvation as explained in the *Experience of the Gospel* are unique.

In conclusion, I can only offer an apology for any inadequacies on my part in attempting to summarize the thought of J.W. Kaiser in these few pages. His work is so finely sculpted that every line bears close scrutiny. He opens a path to a new appreciation of our spiritual heritage. May the intensity of his writing, and his stern love and dedication to hearing the Word as it was meant to be heard - namely in our own living experience of its truth - be an inspiration to all who read these pages.

Sanctification of Life

Do not let anyone refer you to the historical figures, who have been declared saints by people, possibly after they had first been diabolically tortured and killed by those same people... in the name of GOD or Christ. The world that considers itself qualified to judge holy and unholy, acceptable and reprehensible before GOD, is completely an outsider. So much so that, in a confusion of time and the actors of time with its own miracle-constellation, it considers holy whoever by boundlessly biting his teeth into a conviction of the blind Ego stood up to the delusion and will of the world, and in passionate conviction of his views preferred to be thrashed by the aroused collective obsession, rather than acknowledge - out of love for truth - the relativity of all convictions.

What help does a person find, who seeks the Father in Heaven, with these kind of angels and their funeral procession? Not much!

The attention of God-the-Father does not ask for a miracle, because that Attention Itself is sufficient guarantee for the indulgence of all sanctification.

The Father does not demand from the Son a declaration of His Attention for the sake of the creatures who do not *want* to be bound by the Father. Sanctification is not a fighter's prize! Being-Holy lies in the hands of the Father, who will let those experience it whom He calls His Own, when the time suits Him.

The blood of martyrs is not known to any "Swineherd."

It is hard to find, because it is given in spite of oneself as linkage from devil to GOD. The dream of GOD by such a human being is more than all idolatry combined and withstands all violence in the pale desolation that such a person enters and goes and knows of no turning in spite of the ingrown connection with it. With such a person GOD is eye to eye.

Our life is not sanctified by dedicating it to an "ideal" born from our wretchedness, which is what our consolidation in a lifelong dream is, where GOD awaits our awakening.

Sanctification is the transition from animal pursuits of self-will to resistless absorption in GOD's Will. It is Salvation and Liberation and therefore it can never be performed by the unliberated to themselves or their fellow human beings, but

35

it is accomplished by GOD in surrender to His unfathomable, incomprehensible *therapy*. Still He, as always, is the Only one who leads from slavery to Freedom. Modern man is the extremely enslaved man, afraid of commitment, who, out of fear of commitment, endlessly hides and ties himself down, sells himself and becomes addicted.

Hence all this paradoxical longing for freedom and freedom adventures, all of which mean a more extreme lack of freedom. And they all show that!

Not by accident is the city, the polis, the birth place of politics, that symptom of disease that strong-arms society in accordance with our distorted views by joining forces. This line has been followed blindly for so long, that the world is now largely ruled by numerical majorities with no other powers of resistance than slyness and violence. As long as the majority of votes wins, the inferior will triumph over the superior, unless GOD prevents it. Everywhere there is crass denial of the unique, everywhere there is a stupid glorification of repetition, of uniformity, of what is seemingly equal.

With that, the most crass denial of the holiness of Life has become universal. For the respectability and justification of Life is precisely in the unique, the exceptional. Repetition is typical of the lifeless.

Whatever repeats itself is *dead*.

In the ever fiercer, ever more frenetic attempts to make presence on earth tenable for a humanity that is perishing from disharmony and tensions, every step, every decision, every effort, wobbles between left and right, big and small, or whatever other pairs of opposites. And that predetermines the continuation of wretchedness.

Even if we smirk or look down haughtily, or brood with moralistic compromise on the old picture of the Tree of the Knowledge of Good and Evil, we have eaten from it and we are totally in its spell.

There is no question of primary innocence in responding from our in-being to what is offered from moment to moment. Everywhere there is a tactic of deliberation, that varies endlessly from popular worldly wisdom to scientific mental acrobatics. It is evident that those groups of the population who are called religious follow a similar strategy and that the spiritual leaders have always participated without scruples in the tournament for hegemony on earth.

Especially, and this is so very painful, the so-called Christians. Jesus's Word: "My Kingdom is not of this world," has been and is being denied shamelessly by those who present themselves as His followers and who presume to preach in His Name.

We should not be amazed that a humanity that lives in such continual crass denial of the essence of Life, periodically experiences a crisis, an impasse. Of old, people have tried to liberate themselves from that according to the laws of neuroses by a narrowing of consciousness, a distortion of reality to a seeming justification for hatred and violence, in stupid projection onto others of what haunts their own psyche. That peace could be established by violence is a lie that we inherited from the Romans. Armament and rearmament, preferably also "moral" (sic!) have always been springboards from which a jump into what had become unavoidable was taken with our consciousness lulled to sleep. We can hardly understand what is needed in terms of individual denial and repudiation, for such a collective deformation of reality. Not thousand-fold but million-fold complicity of all sorts is necessary for that. And still, when in retrospect it is said: we are all at fault, then we bend our heads in a salutary pathetic relief, of what can only be settled in truthfulness and deed before GOD. We are not any better.

Indeed, because we do not want to be!

In giving in to valuations in the pairs of opposites, for the distinction between illusory good and illusory evil, both always fully determined by striving in a direction of which the "good" or "evil" is not even realized, we have confined ourselves to a convoluted and contradictory labyrinth of consequences, that imposes itself as a tyrannical substitute for living free with a semblance of logic and justice. Therein lies endless slavery.

How could Salvation, or Liberation not rip apart this tyrannical framework?

And how could this ever be realized except in being torn extremely painfully from the rut of all such conditioning?

That is something altogether different from the cult of beautiful thoughts, the flush of ceremonial actions, the conformity with another's dogma concerning Him, who can not be captured in any dogmas.

The Religion which is truly a Service to God, can not be founded on *any image* of Divine Revelation, *or image* of "Savior." The Messiah of all people, all ages, does not let himself be registered in any one historical figure. He *can* not be caught in the forms that the human mind always again conceives of Him, and presents as "real." *He who* liberates, redeems us, is not *known*, understood or led by the very things from which He liberates us.

Deification of the few in whom GOD's redeeming Being was revealed, because human nature in them was silenced completely, has caused many figures to be placed between Creator and creatures, which are obstacles to the holy connection.

Between Father and Son no interfering intermediary is justifiable or acceptable. But self appointed go-betweens have always immoderately proffered themselves and have indelicately involved themselves in the holy relationship between Creator and creature. For that ensured influence and power and that was the motivation of old!

Of old, the millions who permitted such sacrilege out of fear and laziness, have not done the Will of the Father in Heaven, but the will of the demoniacal hierarchy, be it spiritual or worldly, that interposed itself between Creator and creature, and was a parasite on the creation.

Again in crude denial of Jesus's Word:

Luke 22:25
"The kings of the people rule over them (oppress them) and their rulers are called benefactors."
Luke 22:26
"But you shall not be like that, but the first among you become as the lowest and the leader as the servant."

E veryone who has lived for some years in this so-called Christian world and has not let himself be fooled by the liberally offered "humble" arrogance and pseudo-subservience, knows what has become of that.

Just as forever the story of the Tree of Knowledge that is no *knowledge*, stands as a beacon for everyone who reflects on it, thus through the ages runs the thread of recognition that Liberation means the elevation above this pseudo-knowledge. (Heraclitus, Lao Tse, Job, Coincidentia Oppositorum, symbolized in the being of the Hermaphrodite, in the daughter Harmonia of Ares and Aphrodite, in the Lilly, etc.) (Daemon est Deus Inversus). In the same vein there is a sporadic tradition of the insight, that this elevation is a being elevated, because no man can do this himself, but can only undergo it in utter resignation and surrender. There is no self-sanctification, there is being sanctified. There is no self-liberation, there is Liberation by GOD himself in Transmutation, that leaves no stone on top of the other of that temporary building, the temporal person, that is pictured in the Gospel as the temple of scribes and pharisees.

B arely veiled the old book of Job shows that the good person is completely caught up in one-sidedness, in which he has drawn GOD into his debit and credit, the modern Our Dear Lord. How else could he be liberated but by experiencing Our Nasty Lord to the fullest? And how right is the admission at the end, that he only knew GOD from hearsay, but now he *saw* Him!

Always and everywhere the improbable, the absurd by human measure, has happened to those who surrendered to God in Liberation. The Jews who escaped from slavery, died of thirst and hunger in the desert. Abraham had to go to a land that his offspring were to inherit.

But he had no offspring and the land was not given to him. And when then he finally had offspring, he was demanded in sacrifice.

That is the Road to Liberation, that is the Path that sanctifies.

Another one does not exist. When Noah (Rest or Roaming) is to be "liberated," he has to be prepared to do the absurd: to build an impossible "ship"... and suffer the criticism of the many. This old image of "ship" as GOD-given *possibility* to navigate the sea of the deadly Mysteries, we find in the Gospel as well and not only there. Ancient Egypt used this symbol many times. And the Noah-motif possibly has its origin in the Assyrian/Babylonian Ut-napishtim, which in turn was derived from the Sumerian legend of Zisudra. Zisudra means: "He who possesses life force far into the future;" Utanapishtim: he won life-breath.

While the Gilgamesh-epic pictures the path of the heroic-glorious human being, who goes through the twelve fold nature of existence in Time, as a round through the XII Signs of the Zodiac, during which he comes to seek eternal life, because of

an aversion to death, resulting from the death of his compan-
ion Enkidu, the "teaching" of this epic is not in the resigned
conclusion that eternal life is not available to man, as Christian theologians explain, but more precisely in the confrontation of Gilgamesh and Utnapishtim. For while Gilgamesh
represents the uncounted of all times, who came to greatness
with the means of temporal values and out of dissatisfaction
with that, wanted to also "gain" eternal life, Utnapishtim is
the person who was given the timeless life. Given by favor and
blessing of a divine nature, especially in times of confusion
and decline.

And what theologians will not see, is just this eternal truth,
that in total surprise God's Attention makes itself felt and
asks for attention in return, despite the improbable figure in
which HE appears, and despite the unreasonableness of his
assignment. For precisely the fact that it is reprehensible
according to the measurement of human intellect and its silly
judgment, results in man responding or not only with his
intuition.

"Wall, listen to Me, reed-wall, heed my Word!
Demolish the house, build a ship, let go the wealth,
save life!..."
(song XI, line 21 - 1640 B.C.!)

I s this not exactly what always, also today is GOD's whis-
pering at the wall of our physical separation? Is the
reed-wall or the papyrus basket not the same reflection of
incarnative demonstrableness?

But who is prepared, based on such a message to *demolish*
his "house", his hiding place, his bulwark (not in the least
against GOD)? And then to build a "boat," the seaworthiness
of which seems more than questionable, according to human
judgment.

No, *we* do not let God's Angel in, if that means the enmity of
our neighbor citizens. *We* would surely rather surrender him
to the lust of the many, than that we sacrifice a daughter to
the depraved, so God's Angel stays undefiled! We are *not* like
Lot!

But in the eyes of his sons-in-law even he was "as one who
mocked" when he delivered God's Message. And even he had
to be taken by the hand and drawn away from the place to

which he was attached for the expectation of the realization of his life.

How much will we have to be dragged away, if GOD wants to take us away from the places that He is going to destroy?

G OD does not liberate "Norms," nor convictions and confessions, nor bundles of habits and freebooting-methods, but only that in man which is receptive to the timeless Being, but is imprisoned in the shell of elementary forces.

Only His Overshadowing awakens in man the Process of Transmutation, that may be called God's Salvation because that is what it *is*. And the triumph of elementary forces over that Figure is the Passion, but what has been transmuted is exempted from death.

The commencement of all Sanctification is not a grandiose self-determined deed or deedlessness, but the human attention for GOD's Attention. Deeply refraining from the otherwise incessant judging between good and evil, and in its stead the blind confidence that "all comes as a Blessing." That is Zachariah = God is mindful of me, and Elisheba = God is my oath. And what is born from that is: GOD *gives mercifully* = Iohanan. And whoever is "baptized" by This One in the stream of life will always, already partially rising above these "waters," "see the heavens open gradually."

But then this untraceable abduction into loneliness commences immediately, into the "desert" of pseudo-abandonment, in which the satanic aspect of the Almighty promptly attacks the delusion of Our Dear Lord and continues to provoke us, until we finally *know* GOD. Know Him as the Father in heaven, who by means of all the terrors of time gives His Child that Resistance and Endurance, which are essential to being lifted out of the tyranny of Time and Space with their misunderstood brokenness in valuation that does not stand up, into Reunion with Him.

To accept this, not as theory or as history, but as the most essential indication of truly treading on the shortest Path to GOD, that is the commencement of our sanctification, which will develop exactly as determined by GOD alone ... and completed.

How unattractive, no, reprehensible is this reality for all who dream of and strive for the glory of the personality, the cult and elevation of what they think is their center, but in truth is only their idealized *ego*!

Thus it is no miracle that all sorts of "ways" are being propagated, which attempt to hide their own lack of justification in the semblance of tolerance.

Liberation is described as a "cure," and everyone can choose the treatment that seems most attractive to him. Goethe has shown wittily in Faust I in what psychological soil the arrogance, the delusion of magic, is rooted.

The thinking, educated person, who is fed up with his glory and realizes that he does not "live," under the pressure of this crisis comes to the boldly reasoned conclusion:

Kein Hund möchte so länger leben,
Darum hab' Ich mich der Magie ergeben.[1]

It is the old tendency of the stranded person with unlimited strengthening of the unholy tactics to still wrench the coveted glory, where GOD only offers a humbling experience.

The unmasking of the penchant for magic, is the unmasking of the general trick: the flight into the caricature of the Father, just to not have to fill the role of the Son. The simple but effective indication of the relationship of Creator and creature as Father and Child, which has been profferred so strongly by Jesus - and realized - suffices to show up in the life attitudes of all people just what their striving *in fact* is aimed at.

This is the unfailing criteria for young and old, for big and small, for high and low, on spiritual as well as on worldly territory. The human being who has come a long way, who is in a high position, powerful and venerated, is always "Father"-image, in earnest always a caricature of God-the-Father. And to the extent that he is that, he has excluded himself from the role of Son, in the sense that Jesus has profferred and accomplished as the Way, the Truth and The Life. That cannot be discounted.

The choice of the soul for the one or the other goes deeper than any decision. The attitude that the soul chooses determines the internal secretion, and not the other way around, regardless of all materialistic judgment to the contrary. A

---

[1] Not even a dog could live like this any longer, therefore I am now given to magic.

scientific truism, summed up sarcastically in "Die hormonale Harmonie, mein lieber Freund, erreichst Du nie,"[2] interchanges cause and effect, in the way all atheism does. For there is no reason to deny the existence of GOD, unless one wants to reserve *His role* for oneself. And therein the reversal clearly is sufficiently evident!

Realization of Peace by human beings depends on the willingness not to consider oneself as an autonomous center, but acceptance of one's dependence on The Center.

There is no simpler, more meaningful or better term for this than the state of being GOD's Child.

For the affection follows naturally from that, an affection, that is rooted so deeply that it - and it alone - has the power to guard the internal secretion for the decline that occurs when a person imagines himself to be nothing but a growing and aging body.

The affection is the power that enables us to bear GOD's redeeming Therapy, that enables a person to sanction the Demolition that GOD consummates in him, with the long lasting dying experience that is inherent in that, while remaining unaware of the unperishable body that GOD builds thereby.

For the Way to Life is the Way through Death, and the instinct of self-preservation objects to this way with all its might. This force is enormous and its consequences are thousand-fold. Nevertheless man is capable of undergoing the transmutation process, continually on the edge of despair, because GOD's veiled Hand seems to perpetrate a deed of treason and hostility in a series of enactments, which appear to prove His Dislike, His betrayal and remoteness. It is this Loneliness-in-Appearance that Jesus bore to the end, by which he "accomplished."

How much has he stressed the "waking" and "perseverance to the end!"

How much has he predicted that the Way would be one of suffering and loneliness!

---

[2] My friend, hormonal balanceyou will never achieve.

Nevertheless the people who think they follow him cohabitate in man-made rules.

For the temporal person equates consummation with the achievement of a form. He hastens to a form, forever and everywhere. Work is judged by the form! But that form *is* not the Fruit! The Fruit of all labor *is* not a stiff form, a precipitate that is nothing but the result of *past* action. The fruit of all labor is *in* people, *in* their lives! The Fruit can not be determined as here or there, as rudiment or form, which really is only an obstacle for new movement. A form is an obstacle, infertile, for it is dead. But the fruit of human-life is preserved in human life, for it itself is Life!

On the Path to life every person in essence goes alone. Not by way of punishment or voluntary deliberateness, but as a necessity that follows from the fact that every person is unique, and the essential can not be interchanged or treated as equal.

This is the meaning of Jesus being abducted by the spirit, by his spirit. For it is the spirit of man, that abducts him from the cozy herd-existence that conditions the soul. Once again not as an abstract decision or the decision of an *ego*, but as faithfulness to that which is known as true and real. In the kaleidoscopically varied daily staging, GOD offers the opportunity to such Faithfulness without interruption, Faithfulness which abducts one into loneliness, that is to say: abducts one from the collective treason, from the thousand-fold compromise, from the thousand times not granting priority to what *has* priority.

People complain: "I do not see GOD, I do not know His Will", etc. GOD indeed only manifests himself to his Own in a person.

John 1:11

"He came unto his own, and his own receive him not."

The mocking bravery with which negatively inclined people are used to saying: "If there were a God, such things would not happen! Everyone can see after all that there *is* no divine Leadership!," is nothing but a blind confession of compromising carried to an extreme. Each compromise works as a veil before the eyes of him that makes it. A thousand times we commit a compromise for the sake of comfort and bad peace. With that we perpetuate our blindness to see GOD.

Simple and imperishable is the Word

Matthew 5:8

"Blessed are the pure in heart, for they shall *see* GOD."

Seeing, not as a hysterical vision, that can be used to exploit a place of pilgrimage and to bind and fool the masses.

But "seeing" in the ancient Hebrew sense of "experiencing," *living it*, as it occurs countless times in the Old and New Testaments. The pure in heart are those who reject compromises.

The Truth is not susceptible to iconoclasm, or idolatry, nor for a middle course or renunciation. It will not be served by this most absurd choice that is worse than a lie: the compromise. The path towards Truth is littered with tempting images, and it demands exceptional love for the truth to be able to see this and leave it for what it is. The truth is only reached, whenever man wants to be led for the sake of his own relationship with Truth. And when he learns to seek and find that Guidance in the abolition of every *compromise*.

This speech is hard, and reference to our own impurity likely arouses bitterness in our hearts, but truth will not be unseated, but is experienced by all who accept it.

Dismissing the very first compromise that we discern after this recognition, we promptly enter into that holy precariousness, that makes one experience the newly found Relationship to GOD.

Every circumstance and every hour offers opportunity for this experience, but man systematically flees into negation, into contrary staging of his own making. One longs for freedom of everything that seems to be an obstacle for peace and happiness and so arrives at a conclusion of not-this, not-that, not-here, not-there. That is nothing but desperate psychological turning-away, an infantile reaction, a turning-away *that does not eliminate the bondage, but denies it!*

And the consequence always again is: equivalents of that from which one was not "free", despite fanatical rejection and bravado, masterfully crafted by GOD!

We project and abuse our neighbors and the world as background in the silly expectation, that our inner bondage will disappear before a background that suggests "freedom." Thus we move from place to place, literally and figuratively; thus we hide behind big characters and seek refuge in their following as a game of hide-and-seek with oneself and with GOD.

Real freedom arises from inside, and the surroundings obediently adapt to it. The pseudo-free, who allegedly have liberated themselves, demonstrate their bondage in techniques of binding and aggression against others.

Real Freedom radiates irresistibly and attractively, and the unliberated come and warm themselves in that Peace, taking without becoming and profiting without knowing. That is the attitude of outside towards inside.

This Freedom, which, of course, is achieved only by Salvation, is undeniably in and of a person, independent of any staging. For such people have made their appearance and surpassed their dying act in that.

Tradition always works with the enormous handicap that it speaks of inside to outsiders, and indicates the transformation of outside into inside in images that are as much as possible accessible to outside.

Thus the tradition about Prince Gautama, says that he grievously left his young wife and son. The Moon was in Cancer, symbol of bondage that can only be eliminated by breaking it. That demands the "most unnatural" deed.

But which one of us has ever realized that every person, who is attracted by GOD in this manner, *always* has to do just that which seems like "sin" in the eyes of the world?

Who has thought of it that such a person has to bear "the sins of the world," *in faithfulness to God?*

How different, how little theatrically-good, how unrelenting as a choice between GOD and Man this bearing-of-sins turns out to be, for whoever really is prepared to Go to GOD!

Thus, when Tradition teaches, that Gautama left his wife and child, his home and pleasure garden and then roamed from seekers to seekers, but finally reached the Mystery in himself, it gives an untrue and distorted image. For departing from a young wife and a child, is converted by Time, like any other suffering, into bearable melancholy. But that does not Liberate! For always other women wait, and countless eyes can always rekindle the heart rending longing. There is no liberation in denial of the things of time and space, and the countless deserters of this kind, deny GOD and themselves, regardless of the approval of all pseudo-experts.

But when GOD opens a person's heart, it can no longer close itself to Him. Then the soul redirects its deepest expectation from humans and directs itself at Him. In barely conscious self-determined perseverance, the tenderest ray of the soul that a person is capable of, goes away from those made in His Image to Himself, the Unknown-Known, the Strangely-uniquely-familiar-one, who manifests himself as *The irresistible one.*

Then there is no longer a question of exchanging one for the other, and for a third one later on, etc. Then there is no exchanging of horizontal for horizontal, in insufficiency that never brings peace, because reflection does not find completeness with reflection, but wounds itself in incompleteness and languishes in deficit.

Then there is the one time change of horizontal into vertical. And the vertical unavoidably brings exemption, departing from the horizontal and all things horizontal.

Thus man bears the "sins of the world," in that he short-changes everyone by human measure, whenever he gives God what is His.

This is the true meaning of:

"Render to Ceasar what is Ceasar's and to GOD what is GOD's."

For **everything** is GOD's. And only **because** we give Him what is His, can we ever give our fellow human beings what they truly need. Everything else is a dwelling in half-conscious complicity and thus helping to continue the suffering, and misery of humanity.

How much did Jesus know this, continuing to the bitter end with his mother, who, from the outset, wanted to let him be overpowered by the well intended, and with his brothers who condemned him!

Not the Gautama, who every day left his wife and child further behind and who could not be found by his father, because in the jungle he was safe from human coercion and human defense, truly went The Path.

But Gautama, who inwardly said farewell, not as a self-willed deed, but as a fact that he only fully realized, when it had been accomplished by GOD, and who bore the full weight of Yasoddhara's languishing, as well as the full weight of the "paternal" standard-judgment, he went the Way towards Peace. This is the only, only-true Way, that everyone can go. And on it we will all, in deadly sadness, experience the demise of all temporal expectations.

And like Orpheus we will mourn and languish, not for the one we loved as "dearest" in the place of GOD, but because of deprivation of what we held to be the dearest and the most beloved! Just because of that suffering the soul then sings its Swan song, which mollifies all that is and lives, but in itself already signifies the descent into what is past and can never undo the Holy Consummation.

*

We all are touched. To everyone is offered that in which he can lose the prospering in temporal existence. Everything that deviates from the cliché cycle in this sense is a Blessing in Disguise. What is prepared for us as force-majeure, as sickness, death, invalidity and social adversity, as loss of what we perceive to be indispensable for the fulfillment of our life, that is a Blessing in Disguise. It is always too heavy, that is to say: Because of it we can not stay... the way we are. Therein lies the meaningfulness, God's Direction. In vain we dream of a covering counter action, that will reinstate "happiness." Thus we are made receptive, and understand a fragment of God's Meaning. And only the deepest concern, bordering on despair makes us "hear." As soon as we reject this paradox and spin a cocoon of compromise, we no longer see or hear anything. Then everything becomes resistance, which we have to overcome. Then we no longer do anything, but attempt to overcome whatever deviates from "normal," that is to say, the one and only uniqueness that justifies our life, the only thing that makes apparent God's Involvement with us. In spite of the millionfold variation in form, in essence the Path for all of us is nothing but the Releasing of even the dearest of temporal values and the Acknowledgement of the very subtly and intangibly passing eternal values.

To be confronted with a child, who does not "see" or "hear" or can not "go," or in whatever way is excluded from the full enjoyment of spatial-temporal existence to the next of kin is neither "accident," nor a one sided (negative) burden, which they get to bear, but it has to lead to a longing love for "Light," for "seeing," "hearing," and "going," in the deepest sense of those functions, for all concerned. As such this Blessing in Disguise reveals what lowly, subservient role the human physical condition plays for the sake of all those souls involved in such a situation!

In this recognition, in this deep, unalienable discerning of positive, spiritual meaning, a person begins to leave the spell of the Tree of the Knowledge of Good and Evil. For with this he begins to relax the mechanical valuation, that registers everything in debit or credit; that only wants to know beneficial or adverse, favorable or unfavorable for a purpose that is suspended in illusion!

Thus *John* has become active in this, and the person partly rises up from the waters on which he floated, and "sees" a bit of the Heavens open up.

That serpent which persuaded the Woman to eat from the Tree with the forbidden fruit, what else could it be but the order of Time and Space that forever wants to assert itself, in which man has been placed to Demonstrate his Faithfulness to Eternity?

And of course man dies as a result of this getting lost in the pairs of opposites, *not* in the sense of the pairs of opposites themselves!

But in the sense of having lost his *being* in timelessness. With that he becomes one of the "dead" who can, and have to, bury themselves, until he arises from this lethargy and laboriously Goes there, where the unfailing Attention guides him.

*

Man's Way to Freedom does not go along the lines of satisfaction, of contentment in realization of form.

The Sanctification is accomplished in the wanting of all satisfaction, which can only bind. The human soul, which can be experienced and understood as an endlessly-variable bundling of the Twelve Principal functions, is - whatever the case may be - always as the *Twelve* in the presence of the incomparable, inimitable Master. And everyone partakes in the "last supper" with the Master in such a fashion as the combination of these Twelve in his soul determines.

Only by following Him, do we come to sit on that side of the table where He sits, that is to say on the side of eternity. The outsiders see the Supper from the side of Time. And because every disciple fails, they are as yet only partly where they should be.

Therefore they cannot bear the Annunciation of His Suffering, but react each in his own manner with the unrest of his not-yet faithful soul.

The Gospel is the expression of what still happens and always will happen, translated for us as an occurrence in Time. Although in essence unique, it is endlessly pluriform in its execution in form.

The Gospel is the Path of everyone who *goes*.

And the image of the Twelve does not symbolize the past, but the Present until the end of Time. Whoever follows the Master, experiences what he has foretold in the Speech of Last Things. Wherever in the world the Crucifixion is shown, there will be a deep misunderstanding of its absolute value. For outsiders can not understand Inside. It is of utmost importance that meaning is assigned not to the existing expression and meaning, but is consummated completely separate from that in the suffering that is willed and administered by God, not as a uniform quality and dosage, but uniquely for every person.

The Mystery of Salvation reveals itself only to him who lives it and experiences the interchanging of the life centers; as also does *Jesus*, who is not the sweet and soft collaborator with peoples' time-bondage, as he is described to us by pseudo-priests and proffered as the Son of GOD.

What is begotten in the soul of man by the Overshadowing by GOD, is the "figure" of God's *salvation*.

Therefore it is not a historical "person," but just like he has said himself:

"I am the way, the truth, and the life."
John 14:6

That is why no one comes to the Father but through him, because he is not a person, but the Divine Process, the Divine Therapy itself!

Altogether misplaced is the quasi-objective protestation that the "Christian religion" is one of the many. What people call the Christian religion is nothing but the system of compromise that the hotbeds of non-following have created.

But whatever terms are found and chosen, the essence of Liberation has already been expressed in the discarded terminology, that was not understood and rejected prematurely.

Jesus, God's Salvation, the immaterial *bridge* from creature to Creator. Jesus, who is not a dying mortal, nor a one time appearance, but who takes shape as the Divine Process in every person, who - drawn by the longing for the Nameless, which this Irresistible one himself begets - lets GOD's *work* be done to him in surrender. Who lets the point of gravity in himself be relocated from the human to the divine, and thus lets the Makifim, the "lights" or lifecenters be interchanged in himself. Of course this never ever happens as a quasi self-accomplished magical diversion, but rather in lacking all that could give satisfaction and glory. Thus as a true "losing of life," and also as a true *being saved*. And on this long road of suffering only the high and quiet joy remains: to be allowed to fulfill the Son-ship on earth.

Jesus, he who is and is not, who does *not* interpose himself between GOD and Man as first hindrance, which multiplies to a complete miserable hierarchy of obstacles between Creator and creature, but who substantiates the bridging of the abyss of utter apparent-forlornness and apparent-loneliness as *Transmutation-figure,* essentially unique, unpredictable in form and inimitable.

Jesus, who we are not, and will not become, but Who appears in our place as "we" no-longer are, and let ourselves be demolished and transformed into what then can only be called *Jesus.*

For he who "walks" with GOD, is no longer "seen" by those who do not do that, unless in a moment of elevation of the soul GOD Himself shows "the Enlightened" in his imperishable body. But this is not an occurrence in Time; the temporal development is prepared for it. And in this showing rests the Divine Reminder to acknowledge and follow the Son-ship.

J ust as not one of the Jews who entered the desert reached the Promised Land, but only those who were born in the desert, likewise only what has descended from heaven ascends to heaven.

One time we will stand at the grave, and will find nothing but the "bandages," the symbols of the last bondages of the dead. But also that "shroud," that bears the imprint of them who die in this way. Which in its incalculable diversity still shows one and the same, generally recognized likeness of "He Who Accomplished" as the Verum Icon for those who bear this Face as Consolation and only hope in their souls during the gray night of longing and suffering.

The Ageless one at the Grave shows these few the Way toward Life, the last projection in Form towards immediate experience of *being.*

He is The One Forever Watching, who is always present where man would die without his presence. And our longing is not for Jesus, but for HIM who reveals himself in him as *Messiah*, Christ, Krishna!

Only in this Angel does HE suddenly come forward in the Gospel.

HE-who-cannot-be-found, who finds us, because we do not find Him, HE-who-cannot-be-possessed who possesses us, HE-who-cannot-be-coerced who rules us.

What would we do, what would we say if we did not "see" and "hear" anything at this empty grave?

That is why He appears thinly veiled as a minor figure, for He whom we expect on the highest throne, always reveals himself in the quietest, humblest Service. Never has HE scorned simplicity; no deed, no word, no single figure, however despicable to human eyes, has he deemed unacceptable if it can serve for the sake of His creature.

That is why we do not recognize Him! And that is why we always ask Him for the one we can not do without, not realizing that in this patiently-waiting Appellant-to-our-consciousness appears to us the Only one in whom we are safe, the Eternal one, and Only one who *is.*

*

Thus Sanctification of life is not just a letting oneself be abducted from the labyrinth of bondage, from the attachment to values of time and space with its illusions and never-achieved ideals, but also and expressly the abandonment of all Images that man considers intermediaries between GOD and himself, but which in truth are fatal obstacles.

We are now in the most severe crisis that humanity has ever lived through. For many times before have old norms and standards faded away and have large groups had to find a new orientation and style of life.

But never has it been necessary to find a truly universal orientation and a style of life that is meaningful for all. Therefore it will be necessary, that very much that seemed worthwhile and even indispensable, be abandoned to make room for what is universally-suitable. Not only will the despicable striving for hegemony by groups on grounds of self-aggrandizement be shown up until it is really abandoned, but also forms of religion, which all show a self-righteousness and delusion of superiority which can not exist in the One True Religion, will be shown up as man-made systems for dodging *the one necessity.*

Only **then** will man see himself forced to no longer form deceptive defense mechanisms between God and himself, but dedicate himself to Life for what it truly is:

Service to GOD.

The trumpet of Gathering is presently being blown everywhere by groups, which, despite all beautiful, pious slogans, in fact still embrace the means of animality: violence and slyness.

This is an Appeal to all of humanity.

IN THE NAME OF GOD nothing can be countered to that but: the naked reality, the Fulfillment of the Son-ship as the only Life-consummation acceptable to GOD.

Such as it presently is on earth, a lot can break loose that has rooted itself over time in human degeneration, which even transcends the border of animality. The counter balance for this is not in a volume of Revelation, but in the received Attention of GOD, which on earth produces its relief valves to HIM.

May we, impressed with the necessity of our full attention for GOD's Attention for us, respond to the coming development of things by grasping The Hand that Reaches out.

*   *
*

Religion and Religions

> "As the father has loved me, so I have loved
> you; abide in my love. If you keep my
> commandments, you will abide in *my* love,
> just as I have kept my Father's command-
> ments and abide in *His* love."
> (John 15:9-10)

Much of what I am going to say must appear unwelcome or even hurtful and offensive to your ears.

Please, do not mistake it for a specimen of modern warfare with hydrogen-bombs or with heartless words! But take it rather for the knocking of a stranger at your door. An uninvited guest who - once let in - may prove to be familiar to your deepest hopes and wishes.

Do not mind *me*! I am no more than just a footman who ushers in the Guest for whom there is no room.

Are not our hearts like the house of Penelope, crowded with images and imitations of the One Beloved, who, upon coming home, first has to kill those pseudo lovers?

A dark, cloudy night in autumn, nature patiently awaiting winter. Suddenly a cat screeches in the garden and a little boy sits up in bed, his hair standing on end. "How terrible! A baby left alone in the darkness, crying for help..."

This might seem "material" for a psychoanalytic investigation, but it serves a better purpose than that: it is just an illustration of what we all do when we are confronted with reality.

We all imagine that we more or less adequately deal with reality in the valuation we make of it by applying the functions of our subjective apparatus; and although vaguely conscious of the relativity of our interpretation of our impressions, we somehow are confident that we are able to control our inclination to distort and color the image of what *is*, and we consider our conclusion rather reliable.

In fact we all go by a series of distorted and colored images and by a complicated pattern of misinterpretations, and nevertheless believe that we are aware of what is real and true.

The whole of this fabric of our own making is what we call our world view and the more we think and reason and embellish it, so as to make it reliable and suitable to guide us smoothly and safely through the vicissitudes of life, the more it is imbued with the very inadequacy of our individual misinterpretation.

This is not flattering, especially not to those who imagine they have succeeded in formulating the truth. I am thinking of philosophers, the authors of: *Die Welt als Wille und Vorstellung*[1], *The Riddle of the Universe*, *Die Lehre vom Wesen*[2], etc., not to mention the more modern ones. In fact all such representations which seemingly pretend to measure the immeasurable, are mere projections of desperate self-justification, desperate struggles to reduce Life to an activity of reasoning, efforts to stand aloof and look on, efforts to escape and master what can only be experienced. They are therefore essentially not realizations of Life, but concealed failures to live.

But the same holds true for all of us! We all try to master life, or rather we all shrink from its dangers and bad chances; we do not frankly and bravely experience the process of living, but we all invent and shape a complicated strategy, a system of entrenchment, and with the help of these we hope to master Life, to conquer the unconquerable.

That is why we, sooner or later, have to find out that in the end it is never we who conquer! That is why we all end in surrender, willingly or unwillingly, consciously or unconsciously, on our death-bed if not before.

For there is only One who is invincible, One Who conquers! There is no conqueror but GOD!

WA LA GALIBA ILLA'ALLAH[3]

N o man is stronger than his moment, when it comes. And truly, it will come, again and again, sooner or later.

I t is of the utmost importance to understand that what we discern is not reality, that it has neither the compound quality, nor the fullness of reality, but it is merely a fragmentary image to which we assign value by adapting it to our

---

[1] The world as will and imagination.
[2] The teaching of the essence.
[3] This saying occurs countless times in the alabaster decorations of the Alhambra.

existing fabric of valuations and conclusions, and which if possible has to serve to confirm our whole world view.

For it is characteristic of all philosophies, of all subjective conceptions, that they are in constant need of *confirmation*! This means that somehow, deep within our mind we "know" that our world view, our interpretation, our philosophy is essentially nothing but a contrivance to justify our attitude, that is to say our "strategy," that is our entrenchment, our defense system, our frustration of life.

Realization of Truth, be it ever so fragmentary, never needs confirmation, but all theories, all systems, all mental conclusions are constantly in need of confirmation. The so-called proof or demonstration is constantly repeated, just because none of these products of the rational reflection has *life* in itself, none of them is... true!

The demand of a proof is a symptom of something being produced to serve *instead* of truth. Reasoning intrinsically is a substitute for direct insight, direct realization. Reasoning is rooted in fear of spontaneous experience. Experiments are substitutes for experience. Experimental science and the experimental attitude towards life are symptoms of fear of spontaneous experience, highly developed systems to avert dangers and risks, to avoid being taken by surprise, to eliminate erroneous response, to avoid suffering.

Living among millions of human beings, none of whom is a true insider to life, none of whom shows us full realization of life, but who all use a laborious, obviously inefficient system of interpretation and frustration, we hear and proffer an immense quantity of judgment and criticism on collective and individual conduct and self justification.

But all the judgment and criticism in the world cannot produce true insight, true realization of life. It is comparatively useless to see the self-deception of our fellow men, unless in as far as it is identical with our own self-betrayal. It is, however, extremely valuable to see through the self-deception which is common to all. But such an illusion is far more difficult to discern and reveal than any special delusion.

Consequently the continual warfare among adherents of philosophies, creeds, ideologies and convictions never yields real results. In such controversies it is not Truth that is sought and served, but justification and triumph of the specific creed or ideology.

The contentions and value judgments have little value in themselves. In reality, mankind is not divided into believers and non believers, religious and non-religious people. There are believers who are rather would-be-believers, and non believers who are not even conscious of their blind belief in a system of illusions.

There is no need to believe in what is; there is a constant need and urge to believe in what is not!

People do not believe in GOD, they believe in some image or doctrine concerning Him! Others "believe" in some argument or formula which asserts that GOD "does not exist." The difference in attitude is obvious, but it is not fundamental. *Fundamentally they are under one and the same delusion, but cannot admit that it is so, because this would rob them of their imagined certainty.*

Surely, "this is a hard saying; who can listen to it?" (John 6:60). Well, only those who love and seek Truth rather than their systems of entrenchment, can (and will) listen to sayings of this kind. All others will merely resent it.

Please do not think lightly of this extremely strong and sadly effective trick of the psyche, or of the "ego" structure if you like, our centric consciousness.

A thousand times we hear people assert that this or that happened, and from that moment they "knew" or "understood" that things really are such and so... and then they express a view, which they themselves take for a piece of insight, a fragment of truth that they discovered.

What they offer is neither insight nor truth, but a fragment of adaptation, a piece of self-justification swiftly produced at the moment, when the "ego" was confronted with some reality, the acceptance of which would demand the rejection of some cherished illusion. The self-deception lies in the very discernment or discovery, which is an interpretation mistaken for a fact. The unconscious nature of the adaptation makes it very hard for us to recognize it.

It is no wonder that all illusions pretend to be on good terms with the Truth. Nevertheless all people get terribly upset and vindictive, whenever one of their misconstructions of reality is exposed.

This is what causes resentment, hatred and revenge, whenever the Word of GOD is spoken on earth.

This is the reason why the WORD of GOD cannot be welcome when it comes to liberate us from the web of entanglement which we have been weaving for so long.
It is of great significance indeed that the man who first observed this "shrinking back" from reality and the ensuing "flight" into some irrational world of our own making,- I mean Sigmund Freud, who introduced so-called "psychoanalysis" (which of course it is not) - that this ingenious man who knew he himself had several unmistakable symptoms of neurosis, imagined he could eliminate the misinterpretation in question in his observations and conclusions concerning the conduct of the psyche.
One of the fundamental rules in psychiatry is that no one can cure anybody else of the aberration he suffers from himself. No proof is necessary to see why this is so.
Since this is so, what about the "morbid" process that is common to us all?
Does this not suffice to conclude that:
NO VIEW OR THEORY CAN EVER BE FULLY TRUE AND RELIABLE EXCEPT WHEN CONCEIVED AND EXPRESSED BY A MAN "IN WHOM THERE IS NO GUILE" (John 1:48)?

This truth was implied when Jesus said: (John 8:46): "Which one of you convicts me of 'sin'?" For only what *he* said and did was really TRUE!!
It is of this "sin" (Greek: hamartia,which is "missing the mark," failure, from which the misleading word "sin" is derived) that the world must be convinced, must become conscious, in order to be saved. It is the Paraclete (Councilor, Advisor), the Holy Spirit only who can do it and will do it. (John 16:8)
All views and theories are partially misleading unless presented by one who is perfectly pure of heart and mind, perfectly Free, perfectly enlightened.
In all other views lies an element of adaptation of truth to the specific system of self-justification.
This holds true for all ideas, ideals, and slogans! Take for example such "ideas" as "Moral Rearmament" and "Christian Leadership." Isn't it obvious that both terms are rooted in the worship of Power and Force, where Jesus taught meekness and non-resistance to evil?

Truly, our ideals and slogans betray our entanglement, just as the breath of a drunken driver reveals his guilt!

Therefore, beware of Pro and Con! There is no truth in contrasting opinions, although the world is full of exactly this phenomenon. Neither one of contrasting opinions is ever true. Look at national and international politics! Look at the endless antagonism among religions. One and the same "illness" is common to all; all are possessed of the illusion that truth could be caught in any pair of opposites!

Truth will always be the undefinable "third," which - thank GOD - *is always present*, on all "battlefields" of "opponents," in all shows, rivalries and contests of religions with their imagined superiority and monopolistic goals.

Truth is everywhere, because GOD is everywhere, ruling and carrying out His Will in spite of our blind notions of that Will, in spite of our pretended speaking and acting in His Name.

In trying to strive for a satisfactory experience in life, we indulge in countless evasions of "difficulties" and of experiences that mean suffering. And our system of pseudo-justifications prevents us from fulfilling our Life: *speaking the Word that heals and performing the Act that liberates.*

The distinction between believers and non believers is just as futile as the distinction between any other opposing views. Common to both is an unconscious bias.

Therefore it is typical of psychoanalytical atheism (materialism) that it justifies itself by a mere *explanatory accusation* of the religious sentiment:

It says:

"...that man, striving for truth, when confronted with the heartlessness of existence, and realizing the inevitable end of this fragile life of ours, cannot accept this reality and consequently substitutes a wishful dream of an eternal life, paternal protection and a safe homecoming for it." (From: R. Le Coultre, *De Groene Amsterdammer*, May 5th 1956).

You will note the plausibility of this theorem.

Please also note that it is *not* the product of a fully enlightened mind, but a psyche, burdened with illusions and groping for Light under the constant stress of the urge for a justification.

It is merely Freud's wish-dream!

Now if there is one people in whom the religious sentiment has proved fundamental through the ages, it is the Jews. (See

Martin Buber's "emuna," the innate awareness of being in God's Hand).

It is *impossible* therefore that Freud's thesis would be free of prejudice. Consequently it must be misleading and correspondingly appeal to those people who themselves are still caught within the polarity: GOD or NO GOD. This was Freud's "complex."

The same holds true for Alfred Adler and his Individual-psychology, based on centralizing the polarity inferiority-superiority in which he was caught. It also holds true for C.G.Jung, who managed to conceal his fundamental prejudice in brilliant creativity, until his book on Job revealed what really incited him to develop his psychology and his misvaluing of religion as a thing which psychology could master. For surely, if psychology masters religion, then Jung becomes GOD's boss.

I do not for a moment intend to detract from the merits of the men in question. But they are all *splendid illustrations* of the simple but important fact which must be fully grasped, if we are to see the difference between Religion, i.e. the restoration of man's innate relationship to GOD, and the numerous systems of religion.

And if we at last discover this difference, we shall understand that all these systems are not really conducive to GOD, *but restrain us from approaching GOD, as they bind us to conceptions, prescriptions and standard conduct, which prevent us from following our unique path and reaching our unknown destination.*

We all labor under the same delusion; we all obey the same misleading urge of the "ego."

As long as a man comes with a theory and system, he demonstrates the very symptom of being under a delusion. The only thing that is not suspicious is Realization of Life.

A man who has realized Life, will never propose a theory or philosophy. For such a man *has* no theory, no creed, no method, no career, either medical, or priestly, or any other kind. Such a man *has* nothing but himself and *is* nothing but "himself..." Therefore he is "like GOD" (Mi-cha-el)! GOD too has nothing but Himself, and is nothing but Himself. Therefore such a man, and such a man alone, brings the light that is Truth, and gives Life and heals, wherever what he is and says and does is not altogether rejected by the entangled souls who imagine that their illusions would be preferable...

The story of Theseus in Greek mythology is very instructive. After killing the Minotaur in the maze of impure human reasoning and feeling (the monster of lower urges in man) which he found thanks to the "thread" of logical thinking which Ariadne (Ariachne) had given him because she liked him, Theseus decides to take her with him as his bride.

But on his way "home" he gets the divine intimation that he *must* leave her behind in Naxos. He obeys but is so overcome with grief at his "infidelity" that he forgets to hoist the white sails, which were to be the token that he had returned a victor over the Minotaur. So when his father, waiting on the rock of illusion, saw the ship with black sails coming, he threw himself from the rocks and perished. THAT IS WHY THESEUS SUCCEEDED HIM AS KING.

Here it is. Accomplishment of the One Thing Needful demands more than we can bear. It is only in going through apparent failure, utter darkness and despair, that man can come to an: "All is fulfilled."

If this does *not* happen, the old "king," that is he who lives enslaved to the Minotaur, will not die, but will go on reigning.

Alas, they who brought us new philosophies, new creeds, new ideologies, have *never* deserted "Ariachne" when the moment to do so had come.

They all hoisted "the white sails."

They all became famous and were hailed as glorious conquerors of evil. But the old "king" continued to reign. That is: things did not really change.

One man will tell you that he is a socialist, *because*... another that he is a conservative *because*... yet another one will tell you that he got married *because*... and a fourth one that he remained a bachelor *because*... and so on, and so on, in a dreary monotony of justification, where no justifications were asked or given, if the true facts were in accord with the representation.

For in reality there *is* no justification, there is, however, just our fear of other people's criticism and... our concealed uneasiness at not being in conformity with the standard-image of fulfillment of life.

If you let them have their way, they will deftly switch to telling you that you should stop this, *because*... and start that, *because*... etc.

Such is centric man. To be centric means to be completely caught up in the illusion of our own centrality, and as a consequence to try continually to take GOD's place and do His work as we misinterpret it. To be a centric individual means to be caught in the contrast of tyranny and slavery, consciously and unconsciously aiming at bossing others lest we be bossed ourselves. This, in fact, is the keynote of what we call "society." And it is, of course, not the open despots but the disguised ones, the humble servants, who are most completely caught-up in the delusion. Similarly what we call sympathy (and mostly take for love) is merely *interest* of our centric consciousness; it is the other side of aversion. Centric consciousness is incapable of impartiality, or disinterest. What it would have you accept as such, is really indifference.

We, centric people, develop this centric consciousness in the course of our lives. Therefore we are unhappy and never realize Peace. We adopt people, things, and values, or reject them. We support individuals, ideas, and endeavors, or we oppose them. Or we are indifferent (neutral). We enter into personal relationships, and meddle with other people's individual existence; but when the relationship is not what we expect (demand) it to be, we break it off or forsake it. So we continually live in defiance of GOD's Oneness, abusing all and being abused by all.

It is this which accounts for the sad words in the Gospel of St. John (2:24-25):

"But Jesus did not entrust himself to them, because he knew all men and needed no one to bear witness of man; for he himself knew what was in man."

It is this preoccupation which constantly interferes with our going our direct way to GOD; GOD, who is neither a problem, nor a notion, nor an illusion, nor anything which the human mind might assume Him to be, but who is HIMSELF, *which is just what Man is not!*

Seeing that HE is the Great Origin, and that our origin is in Him, the designation "Father" is probably the best human word we can use to indicate His relationship to us.

GOD in no way is "object" except in our presumptuous and fallacious appraisal. For it is impossible to approach Him by reasoning, by speculation, or by any other human method used to get familiar with and master a person or a thing.

If we prefer to build our world view on the assumption that GOD does not exist, well, our experience (that is: our partisan interpretation of it) automatically excludes every discernment of His existence. GOD then is "out of the picture" and therefore all the more active as a factor of "chance" and "inexplicable" events.

I f we prefer that GOD does exist, our experiences (that is again our partisan interpretation of them) contain many proofs and "tokens" of His existence, His attention, His interference, etc., but, mind you, neatly restricted to the characteristics of our image of Him.

For not one of these two attitudes, but both are based on "preference," on prejudice, on personal need for control, based on fear of life.

Many people whose parents believed in GOD, became non believers in the course of their lives. The key to this change lies in a situation of distress. Others became believers in the course of their lives. And again the key lies in the crisis they went through.

All sudden "conversions," in which men are turned into *the opposite* of what they were before, are no real awakenings from a delusion, but mere reversals, mere tumbling from one dream into another. And the sudden "conversion" of St. Paul of Tarsus probably is the most misleading, most confusing case of all.

None of us "walks with GOD." We all walk with our cherished system of individual misinterpretation and self justification.

Are we our brothers' keepers? We are just their accomplices! That's what we are. Wrapped in our cloaks of centric justification, we all have taken the first step towards insanity!! Consequently we are the ideal breeding ground for the development of insanity of any kind. We are the accomplices of those whom we call "criminals" and "lunatics." We are responsible. For, if we had offered them "pure water," they would not have drunk their poison. As it was, our impure attitude offered them no real support, but rather tempted them, evoking their flight and contrariness that seemed to provide a hiding place for their panic stricken souls that found no home, no safety with us!

No, we are not our brothers' keepers. We just put on a *black robe* and play the role of judge, public prosecutor or preacher of repentance. And what is this but a demonstration of our own entanglement, our inability to offer The One Essential Thing?

Or we put on a *white coat* and talk confidentially with them like a good friend. But the confidence is not on our side and we are paid by the hour. And the brotherhood we imitate is professional interest.

Then we proceed to "treat" them, and again our actions reveal our own "criminality" and "derangement." For like the man in the black coat we rob our "brother" of the freedom which we reserve for ourselves. We deny him the very self-respect which he is in danger of losing, but which is indispensable to his healing.

We commit a series of typically criminal offenses. We administer poisons to him and make him unconscious, which we call "sleep." We expose him to electric shocks, the effect of which no one knows exactly, but which gradually destroy his individuality, or we entirely kill his individuality by cutting the most important nerves in the brain.

No, we are not our brothers' keepers, but the keepers of their prison!

We are the Gadarenes, and our brother is the "madman" whom we cannot tame. And when GOD manifests Himself, it is not we who recognize Him and are healed, but... the "madman," again and again!

In a world of such "parties" of prejudiced confessors and deniers, such opponents that are equally "outsiders" to the one universal Mystery, a true "insider" seldom comes forward.

Such an enlightened one finds nothing but outsiders to the very thing he is, to the very thing he has come to reveal.

His appearance in itself is "a sign that is contradicted," as he is "set for the fall and rising of many."

He will have to cope with worldly and clerical authorities, whose resentment and resistance is roused by the very fact that they recognize in him fulfillment where they have failed. His appearance silently points up their shortcomings, consequently they hasten to condemn him.

Only those whose justification-system leaves some chance for spontaneous receptivity and response, can receive the Light that is offered. In this respect history certainly repeats itself:

"Whenever righteousness declines, oh Bharata, the Lord manifests Himself to re-establish the Law." (Book Harivamsha 1:42)

But this *real* manifestation has nothing to do with for example Dostoyevsky's naive description of Jesus' reappearance on earth. On the contrary, it is the cliché-expectation which blinds us to the incalculable, unexpected and unique form which GOD's Manifestation assumes.

Whenever GOD manifested Himself in man, such a man gave an example of his own fulfillment, his personal realization of what Life is. He did not fight the existing systems of frustration, but revealed their fallacy and inadequacy by the essential truths which he taught and acts of truth which he did.

He never committed the foolishness of identifying his teachings with the realization itself, because he knew that *the realization is GOD's own Work in man.*

Such men were the rare insiders and they refrained from doing what outsiders always do: imposing and propagating a theory and a system. They made the Opening and showed the Entrance into the Mystery to which they had free access.

They merely begged others "to follow." And this "following" means to go the unique and universal Way, which all must go. It is essentially the same, but outwardly varies greatly. Therefore it is not undertaken by assuming any formulated credo, by following any uniform system of conduct, by accomplishing any prescribed work. But the Way is travelled in unique response to unique challenges from day to day, as a wordless dialogue with GOD.

Outsiders cling to the outward manifestation of GOD in man. They hardly grasp the spiritual purport of teachings, but record the *words* and the *situations*, in which the miracles took place. Likewise they hardly dare to follow, but they learn the teachings by heart and cherish the books in which the Manifestation is described.

It is not from going their own unique way that they expect Liberation, but from repeating the outward forms once adopted by the Living Word. (John 5:39-40) This has been done all over the world and through the ages. And as this shrinking from going to GOD causes a man to forego any direct revelation, the lack that was felt induced seeking compensation in conceiving dogmas, rituals and prescriptions. The forms these assume depend on the characteristics of the groups who indulge in them, and this accounts for the many incompatible doctrines, interpretations and customs as shown by religious systems, all imagining that their system is superior to all others. It is this powerful urge which is responsible for all religious quarrels, intolerance, wars and crimes.

Nevertheless religious leaders and their adherents go on, clinging to the very pattern that prevents them from "following" and secretly and openly fighting for power and supremacy.

As a result there is an ever growing number of people who intuitively understand that to be an adherent of a religious system counts for *nothing* and that genuine "following" counts for EVERYTHING.

Through the ages religions have aimed at equalizing the unequal; at uniformity of behavior where everything depends on true inner attitude and freedom of expression in word and deed; at obedience to religious authorities, where everything depends on receptivity and obedience to the Will of GOD.

But in a general way the same phenomenon may be observed in all religions. Authorities and adherents of all religions serve two masters. All of them constantly compromise and therefore constantly betray the very cause they pretend to serve.

Consequently a prolonged world crisis has set in, and it will not be found possible to control developments with cleverness and violence, the means in which mankind again and again proved to believe above all.

But *GOD continues to speak, if not through men in the language of man, then at any rate in the Symbolic Language which is His and which He has been using right from the Beginning.*

To each of us His Direct Word comes in the form of the conditions and surroundings imposed on us. If we find the courage to consider our condition of body and mind, as well as our surroundings and everything that happens to us, *not* through the spectacles of standard-valuation, but suspending judgment and conclusion... then EVERYTHING changes.

Then the rigid and uniform "image" of acceptable and unacceptable vanishes. And instead of this, the first, still vague idea of the wise and loving attention of the Supreme One thus bestowed on us dawns. Then we approach that attitude of the soul which Jesus meant, when saying : "This is in order that GOD's Works be revealed" (John 9:3). Then our implicit endeavor is no longer to find artificial compensation for all so-called physical or psychological or social handicaps. But our mind becomes "silent," and receptive to the revelation which sooner or later will come of the divine goal and purpose in imposing just this unique set of conditions on our unique self. Surely such revelation will come by and by, not as an intellectual conclusion but as sudden and direct insight into the "why and what for."

For however sad our fate, however miserable the conditions we are placed in, the whole of it efficiently serves the divine purpose of preparing us for: *going the Shortest Way to* GOD.

This is Religion, Service to God, and only those who are willing to drop all conceptions, theories, systems and methods will experience what it means and where it leads. This is the only true, universal Process of Liberation which Tradition calls Transformation, which then is undergone in the Hands of the Supreme Himself.

No man will ever be able to define this mysterious Process, nor will any personal description of experiences under this process be comprehensible to outsiders or capable of being "used" by them.

This is Religion, Service to God, and it means the restoration and full development of the one vertical Relationship, GOD and Man.

The state of fictitious isolation in individuals causes the distressing impression of loneliness. From this springs the craving for horizontal relationships of all kinds and levels. And it is significant that these relationships tend to detract from and fully replace the one vertical relationship, yes, *that they give rise to a cult of worship and glorification of themselves.*

This is probably the most fundamental instance of misinterpretation and misrepresentation of the kind demonstrated above with regard to psychological tenets and conclusions. The self-interested, isolated existence implies the denial of the primary, and indestructible Oneness.

Consequently all its ideas, activities, achievements and characteristics are essentially mere assumptions based on

70

Religion and Religions

denial and *the desire to replace what is by what seems preferable.*
This holds true from the lowest manifestations of plant and animal life upwards. It accounts for the obvious fact that all such existence actually is one continued "struggle for existence." It accounts for the fact that *human* life too *seems* to be essentially a "struggle for existence" and a matter of "survival of the fittest." Even the cleverest minds have been misled by this apparent reality.

In the light of this discrimination, the whole idea of individual existence appears as one enormously complicated intrinsic defiance of the primary, eternal ONENESS OF BEING.

The myriads of centric "egos" with centric consciousness presuppose the One Center by the grace of which they exist. Therefore, if and in so far as these relative centers deny the One Center, they rob themselves of the one reality that supports them.

It is this contradictory state from which Man can be saved only if he is willing to give up all horizontal relationships for the sake of the one vertical Relationship.

Please note that I do not say "to reject" but to "give up." That is, to be prepared to lose life and thereby save it. That is, to be prepared to Surrender unconditionally: Islam (=surrender), "not as I will, but as Thou wilt."

To be prepared to bear the "yoke" (Yoga).

It is this, which Jesus meant when saying that nobody can follow him, unless he "hates" his next of kin and even his own life! And again: "Whoever of you does not renounce all that he has, cannot be my disciple."

And of course centric consciousness hastens to misinterpret this as an appeal to apply its unholy technique, its perpetual use of alternatives!

Renouncement of horizontal relationships is NOT a cessation of horizontal relationships! It is NOT in switching over to any opposite! It is NOT in forsaking people or surroundings for a pursuit or a situation that seems more suitable. But it is in just giving up the urge to seek meaning in any such relationships and conditions, in disclaiming their disposing quality, their sway over us!

Consequently historical response shows one long series of sad misinterpretations. People's centric consciousness has always made them *reject* instead of *renounce, desert* instead

71

of *relinquish*, isolating themselves in monasteries or hermits' retreats instead of "standing apart" within the network of horizontal relationships.

Did not Jesus give the example of what he meant? He did not despise his father's workshop. Neither did he desert his mother, brother and sisters. He did the Work which GOD gave him to do, and he neither abandoned his relatives, nor bossed them or would be bossed by them, but he left them free to accompany and follow him, as far as they could or would.

So it is clear that true "relinquishment" has nothing to do with any complacency, nor with compromising such as fanatical centric consciousness will call everything that will not be caught in the trap of its alternatives. For compromising is nothing but a trick *within* the pairs of opposites; one exists by the grace of the other.

Whenever a man is willing to become what he *is*, wherever he is, ready to suffer, ready to pay the unknown price, the Divine Process works whereby the "temple of the pharisees and scribes" is gradually demolished and the imperishable Temple built, in three incalculable "days." And all the rest is merely "marking time."

The greatest stronghold of the cult of horizontal relationships is the interaction between the sexes, culminating in the bond called marriage. In its very nature of sublime duality it constitutes an extremely effective top achievement of the urge for horizontal realization; therefore it is also an extremely effective situation for GOD's Holy Therapy.

Therefore it is foolish to either glorify or criticize or condemn marriage or sexual relations in general. Both attitudes merely betray the need for self justification of the individual. And the general unhappiness in marriage should be understood neither as casual failure, nor as a proof of deficient natural selection, but as revelation that God forever reigns supreme in human enterprises, and that He intervenes in their denial or resistance of the one great Task: "to rise and go to the Father."

Thus He turns all such undertakings into His Holy Therapy, by which men are gradually HEALED *of the one fundamental illness, the illusion that separate, individual existence would be* LIFE.

This is probably the most fundamental meaning of Jesus' parable of the Prodigal Son, that man came to imagine that fulfillment of life would be the successful achievement of persistently maintained, separated, individual existence.

The challenge embodied in marriage is that it aims at Unity but maintains the illusion of individuality and its inherent strategy towards other individuals; it remains a duality within the Oneness and it produces individuals.

The very nature of procreation is the maintenance and increase of separate existence, symbolized by childbirth and the cutting of the umbilical cord at birth.

Symptomatic of the insane persistence of this misconception is the religious or mystic delusion that *a* man and *a* woman would ever be transformed into one timeless being.

A *characteristic of Service to God is that it demands and achieves the dissolution of the illusory separate "life" with its centric consciousness and its horizontal relationships that would supplant the vertical relationship.*

Characteristic of everything else is that it pretends and promises to bring about what Service to God only achieves.

Characteristic of religions is that they are not what they pretend to be: just various *forms* of Service to God.

They are not *forms* of Service to God but systems to resist and defend against the very Process which Service to God effects and accomplishes.

Characteristic of all religions is that they are based on a degree of realization of the vertical Relationship by somebody and his subsequent manifestation in word and action, of what only an insider can manifest; and that they all turned such manifestations and teachings into a system *in which the unadaptable has been adapted to the preference of an existence in horizontal relations.*

That is why all religions present a system and a practical conduct which is essentially a policy of compromise developed into an imposing virtuosity of self-justification.

V iewed with the sobriety of direct discernment, speculation on Tao is mere defense against the Tao.

Viewed with genuine familiarity with the continual Therapy by the Ever Present, the training and skill of Zen-masters is a ridiculous substitute invented and introduced in flat defiance or ignorance of the "training" *arranged and imposed by the One Master* in the neglected and misjudged staging of everyday life.

Viewed with some acquaintance of the deep longing for "He that attracts" (Krishna), the tradition of Hinduism and the teachings and practices of yogis are poor symptoms of refined culture of self-glorification by impertinent and extravagant development of mental creativity, deceptively disguised in thoughtful kindness and humble-pride.

Viewed with some experience of Light, the mere assertion that the Buddha would have taught a definite number of truths and paths, is recognized as a shameless desecration of the memory of an enlightened one by utterances that bear the very mark of outsider-ship.

Beautiful and of universal truth and application is the term of Islam, that is Surrender. But sad is the substitution of unconditional Surrender by mere acquiescence and the ensuing indifference, called fatalism.

Truly, each time has underestimated the manifestation of GOD's Will in a human being, and at the same time sadly overestimated it.

No man has been so passionately deified as Jesus of Nazareth, the man who manifested GOD's Will as no man did before or after and confirmed this for all times by his complete rejection of compromising with "the ways of the world," his complete rejection of Power, and his complete Surrender to Suffering, confirmed in action. All others yielded somehow to Power. And yet this deification is nothing but a psychological trick to justify our failure to follow him by making him the exception, whose fulfillment exempts us from the task.

This is the difference between Service to God and religions, and it is useless to quarrel about it, even though that is what they have always done.

For the proof of the pudding is in the eating, and no man will ever find truth by theorizing. For truth only reveals itself to him who surrenders to it, and reunion with the Supreme takes place only when an individual finally and entirely merges into Him, losing all horizontal relations, losing his personal existence, losing his individual "life," but gaining Universal Life, which is Life Eternal.

The Messiah of all men and of all ages cannot be caught in any doctrine or concept of the human imagination.

All dogmas, all conceptions produce such expectations as will prevent us from discerning and recognizing the shape which GOD alone determines for THE MANIFESTATION OF HIS WILL.

For it is this one who bears so many names.

And it is this one whom definitions, registrations, speculations of all kinds, called Tradition, would catch and hold and so would turn into a possession that which cannot be anyone's possession.

This is the cause of all religious enmity and strife.

For where your treasure is, there will your heart be also.

And he who does not gather with the One, scatters.

For Man still judges by appearances, and still expects the certainty he seeks from *forms which the Spirit adopted for one moment for its momentary manifestation.*

BUT GOD DOES NOT REPEAT HIMSELF.

When the One appears on earth, nothing but the unique in us will welcome Him, and admit Him in our hearts forever.

The Open Field
and the Field
of Good and Evil

Preface[1]

In this booklet, with reference to the presently fairly general broad familiarity with the symbolism of the Zodiac and the Planets, it is demonstrated how our human existence runs its course fully under the spell of this symbolism, because our awareness is completely built from experience and registration as values assigned in the pairs of opposites, that is to say from ACTION OF THE CROSS.

That this symbolism of the Cross characterizes the epochs of the human race in accordance with the cosmic rhythm which is determined by the precession of the vernal equinox, is demonstrated for the two "months" of the Platonic year which are just behind us. These are the epochs from about 2100 B.C. and the equally long epoch A.D. until the present.

Accessing the essence of the zodiacal typology, we will see that the highest Teachings, particularly those of the Ten Commandments and the Beatifications, point out that nevertheless in the manifestations of these Twelve every human being is offered an inner meaning that takes him directly from the "wide road" of Slavery in the "garden of the gods."

That inner meaning shows day and night for everyone "the narrow Path," that leads to the Tree of Life in the Garden of GOD. That is THE WAY OF THE CROSS.

The action of the Cross is the wide road, the general clinging to and striving for prosperity, power and well-being, in which the defenseless-higher is always betrayed and killed by the powerful-lower.

The way of the Cross is "the Narrow Path," the Narrow Gate to Life.

It is the Departure from individual and collective denial of life, separately Descending as non-being into the impenetrability of Being.

It is the Ascent out of the magic circle of wanted and unwanted repetition by accomplishing what needs DOING only once.

---

[1] This foreword was translated from the book version of this speech. The speech was given at the 21st Open Field Meeting in Zeist, Holland, on August 29, 1959.

Gospel (Greek: Euangelion, the good news) is what really happens from eternity to eternity, "translated" for us into an occurrence in time. It is not just history, but the shape which the essence of things takes on in a thousand forms, when it manifests itself in realities.

Noi tutti siamo esiliati
entro le cornici di uno strano quadro.
Chi sa questo, viva da grande.
Gli altri sono insetti.
Lionardo da Vinci.

Life in matter is characterized by a striking uncertainty about its course, by its susceptibility to all kinds of dangers to its form, but most of all by its unfathomable meaning.

We have tried to do away with uncertainty by countless guarantees and regulations; we have done our utmost to provide security and safety. We have endeavored to establish the greatest possible security by reducing our existence to a scheme and by replacing the realization of life with the realization of a mere pattern.

Doing so we have desecrated life, and by reducing ourselves to mere puppets, we have lost all insight in the meaning of life.

Consequently we have no peace but suffer from continual tension; we do not respect our fellowmen and other living creatures. And consequently corruption, criminality and insanity steadily increase.

Now that we live in a period of transition, now that we have come to the end of an era with its special character and style, and a new era begins, which enables a new lifestyle, but also demands realization of that style, now it becomes more evident than ever how negative and evasive our attitude is, how entrenched and armed we are, how inadequately and incapably we deal with that which reality now offers and demands.

The truth veiled in the ancient story of "Oedipus and the Sphinx" is demonstrated in us, in spite of the fact that we have misunderstood it by taking it for an intellectual joke.

If the riddle set by the Sphinx were indeed so superficial and silly as the profane tradition seems to suggest, then the event would have been strikingly inopportune in the structure of the Oedipus story as a whole. Then the Egyptians would never have left such an imposing monument of this symbolism; the Assyrians would not have given it such a prominent place; and the Ark of the Covenant in the holy of holies of the Jewish Temple would not have been overshadowed by two Cherubim.

The great riddle for man naturally is man himself, but *what* saves him from being swallowed by the law of earthly existence could not possibly be mere intellectual subtlety. The true "response" requires facing the Mystery of Life. Those who trust in intellectual fleetness seem to forget that Father Time still always swallows his own children.

"What goes on all fours in the morning, on two in the afternoon and on three in the evening?" True, the answer "Man" suits the question well. But it does not solve the riddle. Man is swallowed up by Time/space, because he does *not* solve the riddle, which he is for himself.

The true answer for all men and all times is 423, i.e. 47*9, or Inner Life[2]. Nothing but the realization of the Inner Life saves us from the devouring power of the Sphinx.

The Sphinx, whether pictured as a being with the head of a woman and a lion's body, or with a human head, a lion's hind-part, the wings of an eagle and the legs of a bull, symbolizes the Fixed Cross, prominent in the era when the vernal equinox passed through the sign of the Bull, and consequently the autumnal equinox was in Scorpio (Eagle), the summer solstice in the Waterman and the winter solstice in the Lion.

This was the epoch from about 4400 B.C. until 2200 B.C.

If we are to understand anything of the symbolism used by the ancient sages to express their spiritual insight in things otherwise inexpressible, a popular treatise on modern astrology is of no avail, for such understanding requires the development of our deepest receptivity.

Here lies the origin of the Cross as a symbol of Life.

To our consciousness, God's perpetual momentary creative action assumes the appearance of a process in six consecutive acts. Ever commencing, He creates spheres of forces and the planes of resistance at right angles to these forces, as force can only reveal itself by encountering a contrary force; thus possibility and limiting resistance presuppose each other.

The closed field of opposing forces or "gods" has six phases, all of which (owing to their "half-ness") presuppose a counterpart and exist by the grace of that "partner."

---

[2] *Life* as the symbolic meaning of the number 9 and *Interior* as the meaning of the number 47, come from communications from Dr. G.P.Wijnmalen. The application is mine.

These are the gods, whom we serve for their favor, for the sake of expansion and gratification, which we take for Life, but which in reality are the wages for not serving the One and Only.

We have not been delivered up to these gods, but we have deserted our lofty post, which was serving GOD in the divine meeting point of Time and Eternity in the center of the Garden called Eden[3], where the Tree of Life is.

In this Meeting place of the timeless and space-less and the time-space world there is also the Tree of Knowledge of Good and Evil, that is the tree of Experience of Opposites.

Therefore the River of Life splits there at once into four rivers, which form the Cross. They even form the fylfot or swastika, as they are said "to flow around" the "lands," into which they divide space.

For all times the Heart of Life is in this spaceless Crossing of all Experience, sometimes symbolized by the White Rose, and our human heart symbolizes the same four-way cross-roads for the life bearing blood.

In this Heart of creation Man was placed "to dress it and to keep it." This can only be done by a being created in God's image. A being who has the unbroken fullness in himself and is true to that, although of dual nature by way of "presence" in the opposites.

To "eat" of the Tree of Life is to be a fruit of that Tree, to partake of the unity of Being.

To "*take* and eat" of the Tree of Knowledge of Good and Evil is to "fall" from the lofty position of Being, and to partake of the aggressiveness of Seizing and Having. It means to devour or be devoured, the law of nature. Therefore it is offensive if one does not fully obey this law. It makes people feel uneasy, hence for instance the mocking criticism of vegetarianism. It suddenly questions the selfrighteousness of the animal law with its "balance of terror," devour or be devoured, kill or be killed. And such questioning is never welcome.

In its triplicity the Cross symbolizes time-space which surrounds the spaceless center like a Serpent biting its own tail.

---

[3] This name is derived from Bit-Adini, an Assyrian region on the Euphrates.

That which lacks the power to raise itself, will wind itself round the vertical so as to appear elevated.

In everyone so confronted, paying attention and conceiving expectations works as "being spoken to" and "being promised things."

But the slightest vacillation from the spaceless center means a "fall" into the broken state of opposites. "Tasting" of the fruit of time-space means losing oneself in testing and selecting where essentially there is no choice, to develop a mind which splits everything in halves, which can never accept a thing without rejecting its opposite, which causes suffering by the illusion that "above" is good and "below" is bad, that "within" means success and happiness, but "without" failure and rejection, and so on in all experience.

And because we have done this so long and so intensely, our inner adjustment, our attitude and conduct, individually as well as collectively, is characterized by "right" and "left" in a thousand respects, with a sham-overcoming of this half-ness in an association of Thou and I, which reduces all others and all other things to "they" and "it," i.e. mere quarry, or means or background.

It is this yielding which developed into our consciousness and leads us into bondage by inducing us to desecrate our existence for the sake of Having, both abstract and concrete.

How could Man "dress and keep" the divine meeting place of Time and Eternity except in loyalty to the eternity of his own being? How could he fulfill this divine Task except by standing firm amidst the eloquent "speaking" and charming of Time-space, which constantly suggests to seek fulfillment *where it cannot be found?*

The Almighty does not "drive man out" from the Heart of Creation, but man abandons this Heart and seeks to justify himself by projecting his motive and the consequence of it as a punishment or curse by GOD.

Such is man when he is faced with the consequence of his own action.

Man ventures into the maze of time-space, which is the maze of lust, desire and expansion of the mind. He accepts this as reality and falls under its sway. And then he starts to raise barriers of "faith, hope and love" against his genuine return to Paradise.

He would regain the heavenly state with the means of nature, but none of these means is suitable; they are not only ineffectual but qualitatively inadequate.

Therefore virtues, ideals, good works, etc. do not really promote redemption. On the contrary, all these cause a strained inner condition and the rejected, suppressed impulses will sooner or later violently break forth to unburden the soul.

However sad and upsetting the steadily increasing number of explosions of criminality and insanity may be, they are in truth the fruits of corrupt religious behavior and humanistic idealism, with their unbearable inconsistency between theory and conduct. They are symptoms of the soul's revolt against hypocrisy.

We all do believe, hope and love, because we also disbelieve, despair and hate. Only the objects mostly differ, but not even always. There is a deep truth in the judgment of a member of the House Unamerican Activities Committee. His conclusion was: "We 'have' Christ, but the Cross is with them and if things go on like this, Christ will be with them fifty years from now."

It is however not a matter of "having" and people do not carry the Cross, but the Cross carries them.

The Cross of the four Rivers into which the one River of Life divides, reveals itself in its triplicity as "the Three Crosses" and these will always be on Golgotha, because "dying on the cross" means to be "lifted up" beyond the restrictions of our cranium[4], which is the limit of our understanding, and the product of our "fallen" state and therefore can never be liberating, but will ever more "bind" us to that consciousness of ours which splits everything into contrasting halves.

And as we do not "abide in the Son" but constantly aim at producing forms within the Twelve Fields of Confinement, serving the "gods" of contrasting forces, GOD works in us as the Spirit of Truth and we find ourselves in the judgment or crisis, (Greek:) Ha orga tou theou, which is not God's Anger, but God's Activity. (John 3:36).

---

[4] The meaning of the Hebrew word Golgotha is cranium.

The Field of Confinement promises us escape from suffering by acquisition of power, and we do not realize that this is "Death," that Life and Love are one, free and unseizable in their resistless endurance, which seems to be impotence. For only "the dead" work with power and coercion in dealing with the servile, who worship power.

Therefore earthly power is not an acme but really a low point for life. No heads are crowned but those who lack true insight in the role of power. Having said Yes once, although it was No, they will ever be compelled to say Yes when it is No. That is the price of power. The "mighty of the earth" are those rightly landed in the wrong place, who "know" the symbols without understanding their meaning, and therefore always appear with their presents of worship, where the Child has been born, where GOD reveals Himself in "flesh and blood." And thereby they will always arouse suspicion, which inspires "Child-murder."

Yet GOD will always lead "mother" and "child" to where they escape from this peril.

None will fight but those who have "fallen," those who are deceived by power; they will war against each other, not against those who are released from power and consequently are well protected. But he that resorts to violence shall perish by violence, as he intrinsically binds himself to the battlefield, which is the Field of Power-worship.

*

Nowadays our attention dwells mainly on the forms as the *results* which testify to activity, and we think less of the motive force which determines the energy applied.

It does not strike us that all experiences in time and space manifest a monotonous parade of the rigid set of "gods," whose names - not by mere chance! - were given to the planets of our solar system.

We are not aware of the fact that we do not experience anything except through our receptivity of the eye catching, charming, assaulting, wish-fulfilling, and petrifying looming up of "the gods;" who by fascinating, charming, animating, promoting and requiting, make use of us as of puppets in which they manifest themselves.

For everything in this sublunar world is "generated" or wrought by combining masculine and feminine substances (Sun and Moon). And everything new is coming (Mercury), and it contains a message. The meeting means binding enjoyment (Venus) and analyzing destruction (Mars), resulting in growth and expansion (Jupiter) and shrivelling rigidity (Saturn). This is the way through Time.

Whether we consider the life cycle of a letter, a piece of furniture, a work of art, food, the human body, or our personal course through life, the "parade" of the gods is evident in all of them. Similarly the manifestation of the gods and the preponderance of one or two of them, or the apparent absence of others, may be observed in the individuality of people. The same holds true for nations as a whole; and national histories with their rise and fall demonstrate the same sequence of events.

Connecting we commence. Uniting, separating (fighting), acquiring, and growing we establish ourselves, gradually tolerating and preserving, we hope to survive. Entangled, rigid and motionless, we lie in our graves. The analogy in the sequence of the phases in the various circulations through Time is obvious. Countless parallel circulations of this kind constitute what happens daily.

"The gods are just and of our pleasant vices
Make instruments to plague us." (King Lear, V:3.)

Considering what happens to that not-I, the food which we take and digest, we observe the same "parade" of the gods. And in the light of this insight we approach the significance of Jesus' spitting on the ground and mixing his spittle with the dry and barren "soil." For this act discloses his stopping the natural circulation through time. This autonomous interruption of the natural process and starting of a new one carries the signature of a holy deed, called the "Right Action" by the Buddha. This is the "binding and freeing" for which God alone lends authority.

If, on the other hand, our attention is directed towards the *figures* which the appearance of the gods called into existence by our response, then we begin to discern The Twelve, who surround the One Master in His Presence and who prepare the Passover meal in the House (that is in the actual configuration of things), where the Water of Life has been brought in.

The Twelve Fields offer the possibilities and at the same time the restrictions for manifestation in the opposites. Everything assuming form in these fields therefore has its special character and style. Each form so produced presupposes an interaction of the ideal I and an ideal Thou, as Present, where the origin or Past and Fulfillment or Future (result), meet each other. Thus every Experience of appearance in reality is: the activation of the Cross. The Sons of Jacob, the Children of Time, the Twelve around the Master, the Knights of the Round Table, never come alone.

As fallen human beings hoping for Redemption, as the willing but "weak of flesh" would-be followers, as the mutually divided unfaithful knights of Arthur, they do the work of the unrighteous, erring and fighting in their inadequate "Quest" for the Holy Grail, not knowing that they themselves shall be molded into that Grail, by surrender to the Holy Hands of Him Whom they fear most of all.

For their strength is their weakness and the enhanced exertion of themselves merely means increase of bondage. Therefore the Twelve Tribes were given THE LAW, which - in its very impossibility of fulfillment holds the Mystery that at one time the impossible shall nevertheless be accomplished with the Help of God, (Elieser = Lazarus), causing man to rise from "death."

To each of these types of expression and expansion with its inherent failure a Divine Commandment has been given, exhorting it to show that faithfulness which it lacks and to abstain from that glory which confirms its failure as slavery.

The six phases of creation are reflected in The Twelve, which are the day- and night-aspects or twice six Fields of manifestation in bondage, just as the family of the gods is commemorated in the names of the days of the week, likewise sixfold, but now with a seventh one which reunites the colored rays into the one White Light, as completion and as return to GOD. The same is symbolized in the Chaldean candelabra, the Menorah in the Jewish temple.

When it is said that GOD "rested" on the Seventh Day, this is because people had lost the knowledge of the original, deeper meaning of the Assyrian verb and only saw the negative aspect in the Hebrew word: to pause, to do nothing. The deeper meaning, however, was the spiritual activity which we also find in Lao Tsu and Indian wisdom, designated by "active inaction." The ancient rulers sat motionlessly on their thrones to express this quality of activity. This is how GOD was pictured also. That is how the Pharaohs sat on their throne and the Egyptian word formed by the hieroglyphics Sh$_a$B$_a$T signifies the royal sacrifice performed by taking water from the sacred lake of primordial matter and raising this towards heaven.

This symbolism is very beautiful.

The "Work" of the Seventh Day is: *the Consecration of Creation.* To serve therein is the highest fulfillment of man.

It seems as if the sun moves through these twelve fields and its apparent course suggests that they form a belt or ring, called the Zodiac, after the animals which characterize the fields.

These so-called "Signs" are the mother-spheres between spirit and form. Owing to the earth's rotation round the sun, they offer to the earth a mode of experiencing the sun differently from month to month. And all the time the Moon reflects this light in the Twelve and prepares the way for the sun and ourselves.

"See, I send my angel before My (thy) face, who shall prepare thy way before thee" (Malachi 3:1, Mark 1:2).

The Twelve Fields contain all forms of appearance in opposites, that is: all fruits of the Knowledge of Good and Evil as the reality of our "fallen" state.

They form the Maze in which we err and at the same time they are the Net in which the Great Fisherman catches all.

For each field tempts us to continue eating from the Tree of Knowledge, *but what GOD offers from hour to hour in every Field contains individually for every living creature an added possibility to free itself partly from the existing bondage and raise the rhythm of its life accordingly.*

And because this free, voluntary acceptance of Life has not been done but by a very few, massive releases of mercy occur, generating massive elevation of life.

Our opportunity to respond is therefore always twofold, and what we do depends on our condition, which either still obeys time-space (the snake), or by Turning is facing the Center, where the Tree of Life waits.

In this way we can characterize for every Field the binding manifestation, but also the characteristic response of *the way to salvation in that Field.* By going that way to salvation from field to field the Ring of Repetition is broken and transformed into the Spiral of Uniqueness.

The difference in the life of one who has Turned, shows in the fact that with his response he does not commit himself to a following and meeting of another manifestation of the same spiritual level, but that the fullness of his response lends to the meeting the meaning of an eternal Farewell.

In order to understand this, we have to consider the characteristic nature of each of the Twelve Fields in connection with the Ten Commandments and Beatifications.

1. ARIES, THE RAM

The temptations of time and space generate the illusion that his neighbors destine the native to be sacrificed as a peace-offering. Hence a constant urge to escape his appointed lot. Yet no man can make us into a sacrificial lamb, and no man escapes his fate.

Therefore life is not fulfilled by the self-willed Ram, who takes charge everywhere and always again escapes the sacrifice for which God asks on the Golden Ram[5], which ever again turns out to be one of the many self-created gods, who do not lead to freedom.

Equally the task of life is not fulfilled by the meek ewe, which like a mindless herd animal lets itself be led to the slaughterhouse or the battlefield by shepherds who are no shepherds.

But he who is prepared to render to God - when He asks - that which he loves above all, his "self of tomorrow," even though this seems to counteract the very fulfillment of God's own Word, will experience God's Intervention and will perceive in the stranglehold and terror of his circumstances the "Ram" that really is to be sacrificed.

The sacrifice of our "own" seeing, results in the true Seeing. "GOD will foresee" (Genesis 22:14). In the seed of such a man all nations of the earth will be blessed (Genesis 22:18).

Hence the first Commandment and the first beatification: "I am your God, who has led you from the land of Darkness. You shall have no 'other gods' before Me."

---

[5] The reference is to the Greek myth of Helle and Phryxos, escaping on the Golden Ram.

"Blessed are (not the 'poor' but) the broken in spirit, for in them the Heavenly Order is manifested."

2. TAURUS, THE BULL

The second field compels to manifestation: making visible, making palpable, the longed for and expected; and to the building of a pleasure garden, which always will turn out to be a labyrinth for the soul, a prison and a mausoleum. Thus the minotaur, the pleasure seeking Bull in human form, to whom the young life is sacrificed, is revived.

Neither the lust-driven Bull, nor the sluggish Cow, which lies inert, like a fallow land where ill weeds grow rampant and choke the Word-seed sown among them, will ever fulfill the Task of Life.

But the Cow, charged with spiritual fire (copper hooves), which plows the dead land that is God's Land, so that God's Servant can sow the New Seed, fulfills the Law. (Bartolomaios = Bar-Tolmai = Son of the one who has been Plowed).

Nonetheless the Golden Calf is worshipped everywhere, and people try to perpetuate themselves in buildings of matter and mental images of learning.

To this Field of the Bull the warning of the second Commandment refers:

"You shall not make yourself a graven image of anything in heaven or on earth, or in the waters below the earth."

What else is a dogma, or an ideology, but a "graven image" and our kneeling before it?

But: "Blessed are those who *bear* grief, for they shall be comforted," for He who releases LIVES in the Comfort-equalization, that is Kaphar-Nahum!

3. GEMINI, THE TWINS.

The third field is symbolized by the Twins, because here the dual nature of creation manifests itself in the act of communication between that which is essentially separated. It symbolizes the confrontation of the two worlds in man, of the Eternal and the Temporal, heaven and earth.

That is why Castor was mortal and Pollux immortal; their friendship is the acceptance of life. The Greeks knew that Zeus is not far off, when Hermes appears. The Twins save souls, because in the realization of the Joining of Eternity and Time the corrupting fear of life is healed.

This principle deteriorates into trivial self-unburdening by informing fellow men of everything that causes pleasure or anxiety. It leads to giving oneself an appearance of importance by turning oneself into the messenger of countless tidings and reports; it induces one to speak idle words, gossip, and misrepresentation for the sake of effect.

Abuse of the Word, desecration of the communication principle in trade, politics and the press and in many other fields, desecration of speech in the widest sense, desecration of movement, degeneration of traffic into a senseless hurrying.

Thus the confusion of tongues has spread, while motorized robots hurry over the earth and through the air as messengers without a message.

There is no fulfillment of life in trying to influence another and unburdening oneself, nor in speaking another's "word" or "preaching" for pay, but in Going where God sends us; and not in the bringing of a repeatable cliché as a message, but in the bringing of his Unique universally momentary WORD, the task of life is fulfilled.

That requires the silencing of all human striving.

"Thou shalt not take the 'Name' of the Lord in vain," and "Blessed are the meek, for they shall inherit the earth."

4. CANCER, THE CRAB

Receptivity implies the ideal of being satisfied, satiation. This is the true meaning of the word Mammon, to still the hunger for sensation of whatever kind, not merely the hunger for possessions and money.

Sensitivity implies vulnerability because of lack of selectivity. This Field tempts with a never ending desire to be stimulated by sensations and by jealousy over what is lacking and fierce resentment of all that is unwelcome.

The memory keeps track of a long succession of ecstasies and disappointments. The marsh of Lerna swallows everything, but the Hydra of vindictiveness shoots up from the depths with its thousand heads, eager to kill anything that would liberate these Waters of Life so sadly turned into a swamp.

All this is profanation of the Day, which is not meant to satisfy human beings but to celebrate the Holiness of creation.

And not in any cult of gratification, however refined is creation sanctified, but in Fasting for the sake of Righteousness man learns to accomplish the impossible: to *dance* like Shiva (and Krishna) by placing his feet wherever the Hydra was about to raise its heads, he learns to follow Jesus, "walking" on the waters.

"Remember the Sabbath day, to keep it holy."

"Blessed are those who hunger and thirst for righteousness, for they shall be satisfied."

5. LEO, THE LION

The Lion is the King of beasts, which suffices to prove that the mode of the lion cannot be the mode of the Son of Man.

To attack what is smaller and weaker, and to live by drinking the life-blood of fellow creatures is diametrically opposed to pouring out the Water of Life to all who would drink.

The man who was called le Roi Soleil, said of himself "l'État, c'est moi!" Royalty requires "subjects" and if a king reduces them to "nothing," he reduces himself to an empty gesture, a puppet.

The natural tendency to consider oneself as "the" center makes man like the cuckoo-young, abusing its step parents, and killing its siblings.

Therefore the Fifth Commandment says:

"Honor your father and your mother that your days may be long in the land which the Lord your God will give you."

It is the heavenly admonition to fallen people of this type.

None but he, whose heart has been *opened* by GOD, robbed of the luster of its pseudo-centrality in grievous humiliation and just because of that empathizing with the sorrow of others and accessible for the One Heart which is the true Center of all, will fulfill the Law:

"Blessed are the merciful, for they shall obtain mercy."

The Koran contains a Surah (94, Al Sharh), which reports the assurance which the prophet Mohammed received from the Almighty. It says:

"Have I not opened and expanded your heart, and eased you of the burden which tended to crush you?

....

93

So when you are relieved, still toil
and offer your unlocked heart to your Lord."

6. VIRGO, THE VIRGIN

This sign prompts the native to want to remain in a naive, pristine condition, avoiding the fate that GOD provides as our Baptism.

Thus service becomes a camouflage-maneuver for not wanting to Serve God, and all struggling an attempt to bury oneself so as not to have to live. Accumulation of merit becomes indirect accusation of others and God.

This attitude is barren, childless. It kills joy and it kills life in whatever form it will come.

Therefore the sixth Commandment runs:

"You shall not kill!"

It is personified in all who place order and exactness, merit and outward perfection first, not merely the scribes and the pharisees of all ages, but *humanity as such* as it seeks its own glory in this direction.

Therefore Jesus wept: "Jerusalem, thou that killest the prophets and stonest them that are sent unto thee, how often would I have gathered thy children together, even as a hen gathereth her chickens under her wings, and ye would not! Behold, your domain is left unto you desolate and you will not see me until you say: "Blessed is what comes in the name of the Lord." (Matth. 23:37-39)

Here our expectation is rooted, now that humanity is caught up in frustration of life of this kind and no longer "sees GOD."

For the task of life is not fulfilled by any attitude and activity which earns the praise and reward of the world, but in serving GOD, by doing what He assigns us to do, though it evokes the suspicion and repudiation, the hatred and condemnation of "the world."

Therein and therein alone the Law is indeed fulfilled and true Purity earned, which enables the creature to "see" its Creator.

"Blessed are the pure of heart for they will see God."

GOD, who always prefers the way of greatest resistance, has preferred to be born in a Virgin-soul, in the rare human being, who is not ashamed to be found "overshadowed" by the Holy Spirit, who, of course, will be called Satan by the world; in the rare individual, who does not resist His Coming with all the rules of ill will and resistance, but responds to his Greeting and Word with reflective acceptance.

"Behold, a servant of the Lord; be it according to Thy Word."

7. LIBRA, THE BALANCE

Balance creates the expectation of harmony, peace and happiness.

The seventh Field promises satisfaction from charming, and being charmed. But life does not work with charm and satisfaction.

The expectations that have been raised are not being fulfilled; not the promised heaven opens up, but a hell of discord from disloyalty. Behavior of this kind does not truly consider and respect others, does not recognize them as a real You, but abuses them as means to a quick high.

The Seventh Commandment runs: "You shall not commit adultery." And this holds true not just for the relationships between men and women, but with 'adultery' the ancient Jews indicated anything that goes against the rules of Life. For wherever there is illusion there is desillusion in the making.

The only true happiness and the only true Peace, is Peace with God. There is no fulfillment but in devoting oneself to this Peace; true Peace works disarmingly, just as GOD disarms.

"Blessed are the peacemakers, for they shall be called Children of God."

8. SCORPIO, THE SCORPION

Why would what is offered be something wrong, that needs to be changed and altered to conform to the purpose? Whose Purpose? Why would creation need destruction and reconstruction, according to... whose will?

This Field gives the inclination to mistake any given situation for an invitation to affect, demolish, destroy and replace. But all we make and build (for we can not create) can not pass the comparison with natural beauty. And the whole of what we have destroyed and built or produced has not exactly improved the face of the earth.

In principle there is no reason why we should suppose that God wants us to behave as His rivals, changing and improving

His Work. When I was young and man made materials were starting their glorious development, there was a humorous saying with regards to substitutes then coming onto the market, it ran: "Ganz wie Echt aber viel schöner![6]".

"Progress" has been immense since then. Today our bread is not really bread and our milk is no longer milk, our butter is hardly butter and so on. The air we breathe is polluted with poisons from car pollution and radioactivity, and our fruits and vegetables are contaminated with artificial fertilizers and poisonous sprays to kill bugs and diseases.

Similarly human relations, however imperfect while still natural, have been greatly replaced by social regulations which aim at perfection, but are based on power and coercion, and lack the element of the heart's free action, without which human relations are no longer *human* relations but the mechanism of insect-existence.

In this picture of distortion of the world, and degradation of humanity, these words of Lionardo da Vinci are especially fitting:

"We all live in exile within the frame of a strange picture. He who knows this, will live in grand style. The others are mere insects."

We cannot deny in honesty that we are coming closer to insect existence every day, although we do not like to find ourselves pictured in Maeterlink's "La Vie des Termites."

All this is the fruit of our yielding to the illusion of the eighth field, which forms the focus of our Revolt against God's Supremacy.

We have not accepted what was *given, but have preferred to put forth our hand* and "take." Therein we encounter our "Fall" and we also find it in the Eighth Commandment:

"You shall not steal!"

Life cannot be "conquered," nor mastered.

Our countless efforts to do so are bound to fail and lead us into slavery instead. Life is a Mystery; it cannot be disclosed by scientific investigation, but it reveals itself to him who accepts and fulfills it[7].

---

[6] Just like the real thing, only much nicer.

[7] See Jesus'answer to the Scorpio Disciple's question: John 14:22-23.

And this means loyalty to God's impenetrable Righteousness whilst suffering the world's injustice.

It requires abstaining from fighting death and elevation of our attention above the level of life and death.

"Blessed are those who are persecuted for righteousness' sake, for theirs is the Kingdom of Heaven."

9. SAGITTARIUS, THE ARCHER

Creation is not a target for the arrows of our hunting-instinct, which is essentially lust-hunting. And every hunter of men or animals or ideas, will sooner or later be led into the position of the hunted, by God's arrangements.

Thus Zen archery proves a subtle form of psychic freebootery in the realm of the spirit.

For arbitrary determination of a man-invented system of quasi-spiritual training, betrays gross neglect of the unique "preparation" embodied in the arrangement of circumstances and events made by GOD Himself and constantly administered to each individual. Going the Short Way offered therein depends on our attention and response to it.

But virtuosity in word and deed, developed with self developed and self selected methods, makes us into spiritual misfits and self proclaimed "false witnesses," however "masterly" and "Fatherly" in appearance. (Matth 23:8-10).

"You shall not bear false witness against your neighbor,"

The witnessing in which the life task is fulfilled, is not the self determined judging of another's guilt or innocence, but the wordless suffering of another's false witness:

"Blessed are you when men revile you and prosecute you and utter all kinds of evil against you on My account."

For in this suffering the ties are broken that hold us to this kind of abuse of life.

Prometheus was chained to a rock for having stolen the Fire from the workshop of Hephaistos. The fire from heaven can not be stolen, and this nicely symbolizes the fate of the spiritual freebooter.

The image of the holy Sebastian symbolizes the suffering of one who suffers the enmity of the world for God's Sake. But of course the countless chained Prometheuses think themselves to be moving Sebastians and imagine that as "guru" or "master" they bring heavenly fire to their disciples.

10. CAPRICORN, THE GOAT

Selfishly to remove oneself from the plains, climbing in isolation to altitudes where there is solitude, acquisition of power and control in self denial by rejection and denial of what the heart needs, inwardly perishing because of that tension - this may be called making a career, but it is not realizing life.

On the contrary it is to fall down and worship that spirit which promises all the kingdoms of the earth and their glory, if we do *not* serve GOD.

This kind of glory is paid for with a split in the mind; it makes us into the house that is divided against itself; it makes us believe in form and adore form, it makes us into the rigid person who is *upset* about a deed of real surrender (Mark 14:11), and makes us hand over the Manifestation of Freedom to the authority of rigidity. (Ithkerioth means to be moved and confused. See Daniel 7:15). That makes us into Judas *Ithkerioth*, not *Iskarioth*!

The adoration of form works with many types of obligations, with systematic repression of lust, to satisfy bigger longings.

Therefore the Tenth Commandment runs: "You shall *not* covet your neighbor's house, nor his wife, nor his servant, nor his ox, nor his ass, nor anything else that is your neighbor's."

History is there to show how we violated this commandment and the alarming increase of neuroses, psychoses and paranoia should make us reject the glorification of careers, the many forms of deification of forms and the systematic violence in so-called education and teaching, acquisition of power and exertion of power. To all of these forms of hypocrisy, the religious one first, it has been said: "Blessed are those who hear the Word of God and act accordingly." (Luke 11:28)

11. AQUARIUS, THE WATERMAN

Could "tilling and keeping" the garden of Eden in the center of creation where Time and Eternity meet, ever mean pleasing the gods of the Field of Bondage and being chosen by them to preserve *their* youth?

Yet this is the glory of Ganymedes, the youth who "ponders joy" and is actually "robbed" by Zeus. Zeus who himself is the symbol of the spirit that rules time and space. The "compensation(!)" paid to his father Tros, the Twelve steeds, symbolizes the mastery of the twelve modes or styles of time-space life, which is exactly the ideal which Capricorn hopes to realize, either in the external world or in the world of the soul by rousing The Serpent Power, Kundalini.

Life cannot be gained by any of the twelve forms of success in bondage. It is not attained by playing the exception or favorite, in shunning relations or in trying to turn our existence into a lifelong holiday.

But life is fulfilled when, being confronted with the Manifestation of God's Will, we recognize the Beloved, however disguised. For this Recognition alone constitutes the Rock, on which the Almighty will found the Heavenly Order in us, called the Kingdom of Heaven, despite all resistance from the gods.

"Blessed are you, Shimeon bar Jonah[8]! For flesh and blood have not revealed this to you, but my Father in heaven did.

You are Kepha, (i.e. Petros, Rock) and on this rock I will build the Unity of Souls (Qahal, spiritual Unity), and the powers of death shall not prevail against it." (Matth. 16:17-19)

12. PISCES, THE FISHES

The last Field promises universal peace by constant self-denial, by giving up the foolish striving for personal glory.

It tends towards acquiescence and compliance with other people's self-assertion. So it makes us inclined to retreat and give in, where loyalty to truth demands that we stand firm, thus keeping the Garden.

Yielding to this cowardly evasion results in gradual fading of our personality, that "mask" through which the truth should sound.

This kind of denial of personality brings no fulfillment of life, but *sanctification* of the personality does. That makes it universal, that is eternal, in the mysterious Process of dying and rising from the dead taught and lived by Jesus.

This requires unconditional surrender to the Love which does not take and bind but gives and liberates, and that defenselessness towards the Supreme, which offers Him a safe abode and in return enjoys divine protection.

---

[8] Shimeon Bar-Jona = Listening son of John.

"Blessed is he who takes *no* offense at such a person!"

*

When a person really - however weakly and uncertainly - responds in this sense to what is offered every day, senseless and unacceptable though it may seem, thus giving his 'answer' to the Voice of God (Hebrew: Qol Jehova Elohim) wandering in the Garden (Hebrew: mithalleek bagan) in the spirit of the day (Hebreww: lerouach haiiom) (Gen. 3:8), then the holy Process of Salvation, Transformation and Transsubstantiation commences in him.

In "three days," as three phases, his mortal, destructive Cain-structure, this "temple of the pharisees and scribes," which in vain tries to make itself acceptable to God, will then be demolished, so no stone remains on top of another one, and the Sun- or Resurrection body as the Eternal Temple will be built.

And this via dolorosa contains the three "years" during which God's Salvation (Jehoshua, Jesus) "goes around on earth," that is to say goes around in the Zodiacal experience of man.

These are the "Time, Times and a half a Time" (Rev. 12:14), the three and a half Circulations (Hebrew: Galal, Galilee) through the Holy Zodiac, now no longer dominated by the "gods," but assimilated into the threefold Transformation, that is cosmically symbolized in the nature of the so-called mystery planets.

For receptivity to the Uranus nature makes the tombs of hardened norms and rigid forms explode. Sensitivity to the Neptune nature dissolves the delineated forms of awareness into a fog, that excludingly includes, and in which the Conversion or Reversion is consummated under the power of the all encompassing love that releases.

And Pluto, Lord of the Unseen (Hades = Aides, the unseen), is the overwhelming fertilizer of the soul (Psyche) with the death-aspect of life; it is he who drags down and disillusions the soul to elevate it and release it unto full Seeing.

Thus our roots in time are pulled up, thus the ties that tie us to our human birthplace are broken.

And only this "death" brings about Resurrection, (Persephone, Kore - the Fertile Virgin as arisen soul) and then to activity as Messenger of god (Hermes), that is to speaker of the Lifegiving Divine Word, and thereby to Walking with, Working with, Melting into the One and Only who WAS and IS and WILL BE. (Demeter).

Henoch "walked with GOD" and was no longer seen.

This is how the deceased, who had been buried in Capricorn, in three days dies *differently*, then to arise in three days as the Sun-son and Son of god, who with his "Father" creates creation (Brahma), and maintains it (Vishnu), and by destruction of form (Shiva), unfathomably releases creation and creature.

*

THE ARIES ERA

Now in order to understand something of the grand succession of epochs, it is necessary to know and recognize the main features which characterize the successive eras.

This will enable us to discern essential facts and developments which otherwise remain veiled and obscured by prejudice and bias.

During the period of about 2150 years preceding the birth of Jesus, the spring equinox was in the constellation of Aries, the Ram. Consequently the general character of human life on earth during that age was symbolized by the Ram and by its opposite the Balance, but also by the signs at right angles to these, namely the polarity Cancer, and Capricorn.

It is the Cross formed by these four signs, which contains the main characteristics by which this era distinguishes itself from preceding and subsequent eras, although for the sake of completeness it would be necessary to include the indications offered by the crosses right and left of this principal Cross. But for simplicity's sake we shall confine ourselves here to that chief Cross in trying to show its revealing nature.

In a time of transition it is important not to let oneself be confused by the unavoidable signs of demolition and decay, but to remember, that both ages *express incompatible dreams of the gods*, but that at the same time the Calling of GOD resounds in them, to accept the Cross and return to the Timeless Center, to the Tree of Life in the Garden of Eden.

*

During the Twenty-one centuries before Jesus, man shaped his "Ego" in the style of the Ram. It was not until then that this "Ego" truly took form. Until then (ancient Egypt) blind subservience had been the natural state of the individual.

That man had to learn that there is only one GOD and not a troupe of divine, and anything but almighty entities, has been dramatically logged in the Exodus of Israel, as a herd of sheep under the Shepherd Moses, commencing with the Sun in the vernal equinox, while eating the Easter lamb. Its blood was smeared on the entrance of the homes as a Sign for GOD, that the symbolism of the Time was understood and accepted. The Angel of Death passed over those doors. (Pasach = He passes). The historical journey took place about 1300 B.C., this is in the "Middle Ages" of the Ram era.

This symbolic Exodus from the Taurus period and the story of Abraham's Sacrifice are the lasting Parables of the ascent to holy self-awareness in that time.

For that is what man had to realize, to be himself but not autistic or monomaniacal. That in his selfrespect he should above all respect his connection with GOD.

Abraham's path through life was one long series of tests of his faith and courage, its low point being the Order to sacrifice the only thing which could fulfill GOD's word by its existence.

That was his preparedness to sacrifice to GOD his only son, who represented the promised offspring - and as such was Abraham's own future "ego."

That was - and is - the experience of the most abysmal and closest protection in one.

And without need of the soul we do not arrive at consciousness of our Connection with GOD; we never come to the reality of "Thy will be done."

The Open Field and the Field of Good and Evil

THE ERA OF THE RAM (2100 - 100 B.C.)

(You shall not desire!)
Tyranny
Power/Hegemony... (Assyria - Babylonia
High Priest   (Babylonia - Egypt
SHEPHERD   (Persia - Greece
(Moses)   (Sparta - Athens
Abraham   (Greece - Rome
          (Rome - Carthage

(God is He who leads   ♑   Harmony - Beauty
          to Freedom)   (Athene) -
                                                            Wisdom, Luck
(Ram/Sheep   ♈   ♎ *(No Adultery)*
(SACRIFICAL LAMB   *(Making Peace)*
(Abraham's Sacrifice
(Exodus -Lamb of   ♋   EQUILIBRIUM
(Pasach   LAW - Justice (Judea)
(The Golden Ram   Roman Law
(Sparta-Rome

PROPHET (Eliah)
Mammon (Saturation)
Hospitality
(Keeping the Sabbath holy!)
(Blessed are those who hunger for Justice!)

Four Open Field Books

Another monument of Ram-Symbolism, revealing that we cannot escape "fate," is the myth of the Greek boy Phrixus who "imagined" that his mother had falsified the oracle's message so as to mean that he should be sacrificed. And when his heavenly "mother" sent him the Ram with the Golden Fleece (which symbolizes God's manifestation in the Zodiac), he is carried away, not to "heaven" but to another place on earth and compelled to sacrifice the Ram, which symbolized the very "way-out" on which he had set all his hopes. That lesson cost him "what he loved most," his sister Helle!

The ideal of Aries is Libra as the symbol of Equilibrium. In time and space there is no other equilibrium but a tempered rocking back and forth between a little left and a little right. The tension between the opposites prevents a stable balance. What we adore and seek as equilibrium, is a restless and fragile lingering close to the immeasurable Point of Rest that we always pass by.

The Equilibrium of Eternity however encompasses in its balance all movements of the needle of the Balance to both sides in complete and stable Quiet. This Equilibrium was expressed by the ancient Egyptians in the hieroglyph ⌓ .

Picturing an ideal in Libra produced the receptiveness that led to the shape of the law of the Ten Commandments, which promised *justice* and balance. The polarity was "One God" and "No adultery!"

The Greeks expressed the ideal of Balance in their love of harmony and temperance, in their polarity of hybris and sophrosyne, in their beauty cult (Greek: meden agan, not too much of anything). And the struggle between Sparta and Athens clearly expresses the constant tension between the opposites Ram (Mars) and Balance (Venus). It is significant that this strife should finally prove fatal to their common defense against Rome.

For the Romans were a martial people and their style was a style of violence. The Romans never aimed at heavenly Righteousness; they introduced and enforced their self-invented Justice.

Righteousness creates the unique form which truly responds to the demands of the moment. Righteousness is a living and creative state of life.

Balance (harmony) and Beauty (art) produce forms of delight enjoyed repeatedly and by many.

Justice is a form-standard handled by the power of a collectivity to judge unique events in human relations in order to enforce retaliatory measures, which have been developed according to form.

Rome strove *not* for Peace but for Power. History is there to prove that this is so. Those who nowadays are inclined to accept the fallacy "Si vis pacem para bellum[9]," are reminded of the fact that in a period of over seven centuries the Janus temple, which had to be opened in time of war, was closed only three times and then for a short time only. All "conscientious" advocates of armament should keep that in mind. The slogan is perverse.

The interaction between the I-Expression and Thou-expression was borne by the experience of GOD's Attention, both inwardly and as His Speaking through the individuals whom He hallowed to serve as His "Mouth:" the Prophets.

The sacred records concerning Moses leave no doubt, but that Moses "heard;" and what he heard shows the uniqueness of Him who has spoken from the beginning and will go on speaking forever, Whose speech was and is "heard" by those who were prepared to listen and who were readied by Him for understanding.

That is why Prophets appeared time and time again in Israel. And that is why there were oracles in Greece and other countries, however inadequately they were described and however little they were understood and recognized by outsiders in later centuries.

But the result, the "effect" of the Cross in question, the image of optimal realization of life, under the Capricorn took form as power worship, personified in the Tyrant.

History during this period shows a remarkably monotonous series of struggles for leadership, as if this were the summum bonum: Assyria vs. Babylonia, Babylon vs.Egypt, Persia vs. Babylonia, Persia vs. Greece, Sparta vs. Athens, Rome vs. Greece, Rome vs. Carthage, and finally the Western and Eastern Roman Empire.

The fall of all of these centers of power was caused by the lust for power itself. The general softening and effeminacy

[9] If you want peace, prepare for war.

(Athens, Rome, Byzantium) by indifference through over-saturation (Mammon) have improperly been identified as the cause of decline and fall for all ages. They are typical of this period and are symbolized in Libra. But for our Pisces era, decline is prepared by the idolizing Virgo themes: the cult of the Blessed Virgin Mary, exact knowledge, materialism, rigid social structures, the cult of health, *barrenness*.

*

THE PISCES ERA

As the transition from the Bull Era to the Ram Era caused a serious crisis in the nations then existing, which is reflected in the centuries of confusion in the history of Egypt, so the transition to the Era of Pisces was marked by a period of destruction and chaos, beginning with the fall of Jerusalem. The same applies now, as the Pisces era draws to a close.

In every transition mankind staggers and feels itself threatened with complete ruin.

It would not find the new mode of living, if God's guiding Attention did not constantly help it and enable it to adapt itself to the new style.

In each transition there is an outpouring of grace, a sowing of Seed for the new manifestation of life on earth, which sets the tone of the new style, and enables man to participate in response.

Manifesting Himself in Jesus, GOD appeared as the Opener of the Way of the New Cross, and Jesus' achieving the sanctification of the human personality and demonstrating man's relation to God in fulfilling his Sonship, taught that man cannot live by bread alone (which is exactly the danger implied in the Virgin as an ideal) and he indicated as the vocational activity of his followers the Healing of the Sick (Sagittarius) and the preaching of The Word (Gemini).

In this manner the symbolic values of the new Cross were placed in the center of human consciousness.

The spring equinox in Pisces actualized the voluntary transformation of the "self," its being raised to universality. It established the Virgin as the symbol of the new ideal, which is perfect social order, analytical science, matter-worship, over-accentuation of labor, health and hygiene. Gemini at the Nadir indicated the Word as the basis of the new civilization, communication, imparting of knowledge, and traffic. Sagittarius at the Zenith pointed to the Wise and Fatherly Man, the Wise Leader, as the image of the optimum to be realized.

Promptly mankind responded to these new openings in an absurd manner. Instead of true sanctification of the person, colorless mass movement manifested itself and ofcourse now, at the end, in exaggeration of concealed despair, enforcing itself as a norm in rejection of the higher, venerable. The Father-manifestation crystallized in a long succession of Popes, who carried ad absurdum what could have been pleasing to God.

Not The Word was preached, but with words competing mental images concerning The Word, concerning world views and philosophy were propagated. And with words, merchandise and political delusions were propagated.

What could have been a sanctifying means of communication between God and man, degenerated into a merciless weapon, into divisive, deforming gibberish.

Forgotten was the old Commandment, regarding using the word in vain, acquiring and disseminating knowledge was and is adored; traffic became a cult, the vehicle became an idol. It became the norm to move almost meaninglessly from one known place to another, but the places are no longer known (Gemini). Everyday millions rush to their work and back to their homes with no "message" but gossip and censored news. The world press does not serve the distribution of information, but it serves the interests of the political, religious and industrial mighty of the earth. Everywhere there is destruction of conscience.

The "Wise Father" became caricature: Santa Claus.

Responding to the influence of Sagittarius, we have migrated on a large scale; we have undertaken crusades and voyages of discovery, we have waged terrible religious wars, wars of conquest and of independence. We have generally acted as if Bread and all it stands for were the first and last thing. We have made a religion out of the social system and we do everything possible to rob life's vicissitudes of their meaning and effect by countless measures of compensation and equalization.

We have established "order," until our existence is choking us and especially the young; until everywhere unfathomable disorder and upsetting criminality break right through the incantations and ideological shields of church, politics or humanism; until instead of the sanctified, universal personality, we have developed the robot, the faceless passepartout (Virgo).

We have realized nothing of the "meekness," which would make us inherit the earth, nor the "purity of heart," that would make us see GOD.

We kill immoderately men, animals, and plants in order to conquer the earth and to hold what we have conquered. We "kill" life wherever we meet it, and the prophets are declared insane or confined, because they are a danger to the "state." We "stone" everything that GOD sends us, but which does not suit us (Virgo). We deny sexuality, but venerate Mary.

And because of all this frustration, tensions steadily increase and grow intolerable. That is why the complications have been unsolvable for a long time and the threat of destruction by explosions of raw violence grows ever greater. Human existence has been degraded to a concealed state of bondage, many faceted uniformity.

That is why our foothold is sinking away in a stream of pseudo virtue and pseudo perfection, and humanity is separating in two aspects of one grandiose failure regarding GOD and His Intentions.

Therefore we have lost the respect for life and for the living. We only respect excessive achievements, and are fearful only of all Power.

Therefore there is once again a consummation of time.

*

THE ERA OF PISCES (about 100 B.C. - 2000)

(You shall not bear false witness!)
(Blessed are you when men revile you for My sake)
Religious wars
Migration
Crusades   Religious prosecution
Explorations   Inquisition
Conquests   Iconoclasm
Wars of Independence)
          Hunter - Emigration
          Guru
          Santa Claus
          FATHER - Church fathers - Popes

FISHERMAN   *(Thoushalt not kill!)*
Pisces   VIRGIN-Mother
 Universality   Bread, Matter,
 Collectivity   Materialism, Hygiene,
 Mass-activation   Brand Name Pharmaceuti-
 The Revolt of the   cals, Analysis, Science Tech-
       Masses   nology, Classificaton, Social
                                       Law, Specialization
(Sanctification of   *(Blessed are the pure of heart*
the person!)   *for they shall see God)*

                    CHILD
                  The Word
        Communication, Traffic,
        (Printing, Instruction, Religious propaganda and wars,
        Traffic, Mail, Telegraph, Telephone, Radio, Television)

        (Thou shalt not take the Name of the Lord in vain!
        Blessed are the meek, for they shall inherit the earth.)

109

And just because this is so, GOD's Intercession is imminent. Again "His Word" will make itself heard and thereby save humanity. A new and higher level of life shall be opened, on which its expression under the new Cross can take shape, thanks to the New Seed being sown.

If we are to understand anything at all of the nature and effect of this intercession, we have to stop our restless struggle for the realization of some ideal; we have to focus our attention on the fundamental meaning of the Cross, on the meaning of Paradise and of man's exile, on the mystical meaning of Abraham's Sacrifice of "the Ram," and on the purport of Jesus' Sanctifying Fulfillment.

We should not handle doctrinal conclusions regarding these, but we should open ourselves to the living reality embodied in these symbolic phenomena, which can only be known by experience.

If yielding to the promises of Time-Space was our "Fall," which implied leaving our lofty post in the center of creation, then our return to that space-less Center means Redemption and Resurrection.

If moving the point of gravity towards the realization of time-space values caused our exile and bondage, then the Reversion of our soul's attention towards the timeless, space-less Center, means the true Conversion, which is resurrection.

For all men and for all ages, rising and going towards the Center which is the Center of the Cross, is the only *Way to Life.*

For to live is not to exert and exhaust oneself in the closed field of influence of the gods.

To live is to till and keep the Garden of the Tree of Life, where the River of Life is not yet divided.

To live is to take up the Cross and descend towards self-undoing, as the departure from the playgrounds of the gods and the entry into the no-man's land that surrounds the spaceless OPEN FIELD.

To Live is to meet the Angel with the Sword with deep confidence, its edge kills only that part of us that can not be redeemed because of our bowing in service of the gods. There is no Last Judgment but this discernment between what is and is not acceptable to GOD.

Eternity is timeless and space-less.

That which is eternal is neither East nor West, neither North nor South, neither high nor low.

It is nowhere, because it is everywhere and always Here and Now.

As opposed to the losing of oneself in East or West, North or South, as opposed to the fatal dispersion or diaspora of mankind, there is the ekklesia (Greek, common translation "church") or "gathering together" in the one Holy Community, which is not some organization invented by human arrogance and ignorance, rooted in monopolistic self-glorification and seeking self-preservation by the means of this world, but which is the condition of Meeting and merging with the Only One who IS.

Resurrection therefore requires the renunciation of everything that is gratifying in East and West, in North and South. For all satisfaction of that kind implies the denial and rejection of the counterparts by the grace of which they exist.

Therefore especially achieving and succeeding is... Maya. (Sanskrit: illusion)

And because this is so, every overruling event and situation manifesting itself in the relations between East and West, North and South, high and low, conversely is the signature of fundamental consummation concerning the mystery of life.

If nowadays East and West, North and South can no longer ignore each other, but are compelled to reckon with each other, if they are obliged to "see" each other, if one nation has been literally cut in two, and East and West stand face to face, even in the heart of that country, this has certainly not been arranged by human wisdom and foolishness, but by God, to put an end to premature selfsufficiency on both sides.

But then this means that GOD is putting an end to the silly and premature conceit of East and West.

Then Kipling's lines about the meeting of East and West have come true, and we now stand at God's great Judgment seat.

This means that we are not only compelled to see each other, but that we also have to *listen* to each other and to find a language understood by all. It means that Brotherhood has become an unavoidable task.

It means that the Supreme has interceded in our unhappy struggle about the triumph of East or West, and South or

North. We do not only see one another, but He is looking in our faces and we in His in a precarious encounter.

This is what happens now.

GOD manifests Himself in visibly imposing the supremacy of His Will.

And we, who would not follow Jesus to this Meeting Point, have been girded and carried by God "where we did not wish to go."

For it is not true that we have followed Jesus, that we have really done, what he enjoined us to do. We have praised him, and in hours of distress we have appealed to the Spirit that moved him. But we have turned his teachings into a whitewashed grave. In this respect Christianity does not distinguish itself essentially from the fossilized forms of other great teachings, originally meant to cause rivers of living water to flow from human hearts.

It is an infamous fallacy to pretend that Jesus has "redeemed our sins" and that it would suffice for us to praise him to enter the Kingdom of the Heavens painlessly.

The life that Jesus showed and lived has been replaced in Christendom by a bundle of mental constructs about God, Jesus and life and by a code of conduct, that has nothing to do with salvation, but is a defense *against* Life and Salvation.

True, many people have suffered death *for* their convictions, but not for Jesus and his Teaching. There are fanatics in all religions and ideological systems. Fanaticism is an element of delusion and uniform-wearers are denying their essence.

But Jesus was not fanatical and did not call for anyone to become fanatical and uniform, but he was radical and he called for unique radicalism. He did not die because he rigidly stuck to some *idea or doctrine,* but because he manifested God's Will, doing what he saw God do, and speaking as he heard God speak. (John 5:19, 8:26). That indeed leads to (inner) "dying on the Cross." And because Jesus was crucified thus, but Christians and non-Christians are not, and this path is nevertheless embedded in the structure of creation, Crucifixion awaits us... and has commenced.

For that purpose we have been brought to "where we would not go."

We will be crucified, that is "pulverized," because we can not be liberated any other way, and the constraining ties that suffocate life and are the consequence of our continued "Fall," prosper along animal principles.

It sounds so nice, when we translate: (Matth. 11:29) "Take my yoke upon you and learn from me; for I am gentle and lowly in heart." We have made Jesus harmless by turning him into the sugary idealist pictured by Renan, Thorwaldsen and others. Now and then we do our best to act as if we were "meek and humble." But all this has nothing to do with Jesus and his teachings! For he did not at all mean some nice attitude and the translation in question leaves no trace of his real words and intention, except for the fact that he obviously quoted Isaiah 57:15 and so we are not pinned down to the later Greek wording of the gospel, but we have the Hebrew wording and this leaves no room for compromise, although its usual translation shows the same distortion towards moral attitude. The original denotes a state of the soul; it speaks of the despondent and the humbled, those who are *crushed* i.e. broken in spirit and on the downgrade in life.

It would indeed be ridiculous to promise *revivification* of spirit to the meek and humble, but in Isaiah God promises to revive the spirit of the humbled and the heart of the despondent. And it is to this that Jesus refers.

The dissolution of this expanding-prospering, of which the expanding growths in the body are the manifestation, causes deep suffering but "saves" humanity from its suicide and opens the potential for a new more humane existence.

This is what is going on now and will become clearer by the day. We can not be recognized by our love for each other, but by sticking together in the comradery of group-interest.

Whilst we wrestle with conflicts and insoluble problems, whilst we entangle ourselves ever more, as we introduce our personal and group interests in everything; whilst we resort to weapons which do not only destroy the "enemy," but ourselves as well, whilst human relations have deteriorated to the shameless principle of an all around "balance of terror," and fear rules our conduct, GOD manifests Himself in our midst.

Not as a winged angel in white garments or as a kindhearted old gentleman, but as the Supreme Disposer of insurmountable difficulties and overpowering situations. As the one we fear most. It is absolutely necessary to turn away from blind expansion, absolutely necessary to reckon with others, to try and cooperate for the sake of all.

It is an absolute necessity to turn away from the hunter's tactics of conquering and taking in time and space; in order to turn our full attention towards the dreaded Center, where alone flowers the White Rose.

For there GOD has appeared and there He manifests Himself, as before, *in His Work.*

And at the same time no necessity at all, but perfect freedom to carry on stubbornly, and exclude ourselves, not taking part in the divine renewal Process, making ourselves into the superfluous that destroys itself.

At first we only notice the emptiness of the slogans, behind which a large part of humanity hides now more than ever. To begin with we see standards and principles lose their authority. The "style" is being discarded.

At first we notice that things do not go the way the powerful want, and that the evil ascribed to others reverts to the perpetrator like a boomerang. At first we notice unthinking and revengeful destruction, forcing of unnatural regimes, founded on envy and hunger for power. At first we see violence to body and psyche and crass lack of respect for life and the living. The herd wants no sanctification of personality, but equal treatment and uniformity like a factory product, democratic, fascist, or communist. But in suffering, horror and desperation GOD's goal is accomplished, the deep Reversion of the soul. Not (like the Greek word *metanoia* has been misunderstood) as an idealistic resolution, as a consciously trained mental and moral attitude, but as the breakthrough of an unconsciously accomplished "*Being* different," as a rediscovery of the higher self.

That is what we are led to against our will; we are being *turned around* with our face towards the Crossing and we return to the Garden with the Tree of Life.

No thought or feeling, no act whatever, born from the common misinterpretation of reality in pairs of opposites (that is according to the Knowledge of Good and Evil), will ever bring us one step closer to "the Way, the Truth and the Life."

On that basis all that idealistic striving, all pious and unpious trying to be "good" and to do good is seen as not serving the One Goal.

This is shocking.

This has to meet with the most intense and bitter rejection and resistance, especially from those institutions who think they know "the Way, the Truth and Life," to serve it and encourage it by their teachings and their social and political activities.

But that does not make it less true!

On the contrary, just because of its truthfulness it stands *apart*, and outside the battlefield of human endeavors.

For all of these activities, worldly as well as "spiritual," are born from tensions in the soul and rooted in the urge to conquer one with the other, always identifying one with "good" and the other with "evil."

Therefore all of these activities are "fruits" of the Knowledge of Good and Evil, therefore fruit of the "Forbidden Fruit," and therefore exactly that which makes man leave the Peace of the Garden!

With all our good intentions we clean no more than the outside of the cup, and we think we are deserving achievers, but in reality we are "whitewashed graves." With all our idealism and our striving for goodness we are hypocrites before Jesus, who do not want to "enter" into the heavenly order and who prevent those who want to from going in.

And the eruptions of hatred, violence and cruelty prove time and time again, that the Kingdom does not come with the external aspect, with our striving for a form. And in this light we can understand that the whores and publicans of all times will precede us, "high priests and eldermen" *of whatever system*, into the Kingdom.

With respect to the Way, the Truth and the Life, it is never about taking any positions, never about any pro and con in the pairs of opposites. With that, people make themselves into the dead who have to bury themselves, but who always want to drag the living into that.

That is what holds us back from following Jesus, and this is what he has described once and for all in crass terms.

Again and again his disciples and adherents tried to involve him in their problems and entanglement in the opposites, their imagined rights and obligations.

Again and again he rejected this reduction of reality to a lifeless alternative! He always called their attention to the one living meaning of the moment, the understanding, which is liberating, because it is above the opposites, and redeems man by lifting him above that.

"Rabbi, who sinned, this man or his parents, that he was born blind?" (John 9:2)

This is still our way of looking at things and judging, not only in daily life, but also in scientific research, in courts of justice, in medical treatment, in education and social work.

Far above this level of good and evil, cause and effect, reward and punishment, stands for all times Jesus' answer:

"(It was) not that this man sinned, or his parents, but that the works of God might be made manifest in him."(John 9:2)

The one true meaning leads out of the entanglement in appraisals of right and left, and raises us above the meager logic of etiology and teleology, above the level of dead argumentation. The one true meaning is never directed towards expansion, but towards Meeting GOD.

This is the One Thing Needful, to which Jesus constantly referred. It is often represented, as if he inconsiderately called people away from their natural duties. His contemporaries misunderstood his action in the same manner; therefore they called him insane or possessed by the devil, a rioter and misleader of the masses, etc.

For it is hard to understand, that the Cross can only be borne, lest a person accepts the disapproval that goes with not letting oneself be borne by the Cross, that is to say: that one does not give priority to the fields of influence of the gods.

He who obeys the Cross, obeys the time-space world and cannot keep the Garden of Eden; that can only be done by one who is faithful to the supremacy of eternity.

This is the reason for Jesus' warning: "If the world hates you, know that it has hated me before it hated you" (John 15:18).

To see the true, liberating Meaning of things demands another "seeing," a seeing that is free from equalizing judgment of categorical valuation, a seeing that is not blinded by the tangle of earthbound argumentation.

That is why it demands a long preparation of "fasting" in abstinence from judgment and conclusion.

"Judge not!"

For in every judgment we bind ourselves to the steel grid of false determination, which ignores the one sacred meaning. But refraining from judgment causes the "cataract" in our eyes to be dissolved slowly and gradually.

The broken state of our natural consciousness reduces the holy reality to a Maya of Good and Evil. Therefore confrontation with reality must necessarily cause a dilemma. It seems as if Heaven makes *unreasonable* demands and threatens our meritorious achievements in East and West, North and South. God appears to us as an unwelcome guest.

GOD's Call always comes at an inconvenient hour. His invitation to come and partake of His Banquet will always reach us, when we "must" go out to see the field we have bought, or when we are about to examine the oxen we have bought, or when we have married a wife for those are the "facts" that govern our lives (Luke 14:15-24). We feel completely responsible because of that. And so we are, but only in the sphere of men, whose lives are crippled by valuations in terms of good and evil. We are called away from that, but we always bring up our facts and circumstances against Him as a shield, and hide behind them.

This reasoning consciousness of ours by which we constantly endeavor to achieve, to acquire, to hold and to fulfill, from which we even expect Salvation, makes us blind and deaf, lame and possessed.

This cliché-judging of given situations makes it impossible to see through the veil of East-West, North and South, to the golden thread of meaning.

We cannot *imagine* (and therefore not believe!) that our "eyes" must be covered, that it must be made impossible for us to continue this pseudo-seeing of discerning right and left, above and below, to finally give true Vision a chance. We literally have to be forced to lift our eyes (Greek: anablepoo) to real Insight.

Listening to the countless false messages has made us deaf. When God addresses us to save us, Messiah, Ben-Joseph, God's Salvation *must* intervene, put His fingers into our ears and prevent us from hearing the awful noise outside in order to make us receptive, penetrable and comprehending (Greek: ethphata!, dianoichtheti!) for the Message from God.

The desecration of our activity, as we are bound to the framework of conditioned action, has caused our "hand" to wither. And it will not be restored to soundness, until we leave the inhibiting arrogance of dead institutions for what it is, and step into the Center, from where God's Saving Voice calls us in spite of withholding considerations.

We are the "courtier" whose back has bowed too willingly to human power and whose future "self" therefore lacks vital power. We are "the paralyzed" and the hypocritical entourage of the master prevents us from approaching Him; we lie woefully in the misunderstood situations of Divine Pity (Bethesda); we are possessed by visions of power, lust or fear, we are in many ways "in extremis" and we pray for Help.

But we do not realize that loyalty to God requires that we remain upright like a pillar amidst the powers of the world, which try to pull us down. We do not understand that the Master uses the sham-followers around Him to compel us to approach Him outside that sphere of hypocrisy, to be let down through the "roof" of self-sufficiency and to lie helplessly at His feet. We do not understand that waiting "38 years" is the spiritual equivalent of the symbolic "wandering in the desert" by the Jews, *after* Edom had refused them passage; still it is sufficiently symbolical, this generation long wait in Kadesh Barnea (the sacred wilderness), where the hidden rebellion takes shape and where the rebellious one (Miriam) is buried!

Nor do we realize that our soul, having come to the measure of "things" (daughter of Jairus, 12 years of age) *is like dead*, because the "father"-in-us, getting desperate, implores God's Help, but being an official of form-worship (synagogue) would prescribe what He should do, whilst the "mother"-in-us has been bleeding internally ever since the child was born, but only wants to be cured by touching the outer garment of the Saving Appearance. Thus we have to experience, that God's Saving works "differently" and is not held up by any "delay;" and that secretly touching is not a Meeting, but confessing "the whole truth" is. But even then we shall have to go through the agony of a seeming "all in vain" whilst He bears the scorn of the world, before He actually raises our soul from the dead and so confirms and hallows the name of the "father" Jairus, which means GOD WAKES UP.

Thus He leads the father and the mother in us, who, by their desperation, in need have come to God's Savior, to receptivity that heals, back to the "child" that is in a state of suspended animation, which is Easter-thought of the presence of the "mother" *in* the "house" and which cannot do without the *living* God-connectedness of the "father," but then "arises" from the dead and can go.

We are that "child."

No man *can* fulfill The Law. Nobody can answer the requirements of the Beatifications. The Law is no "duty" and the Beatifications are no rules and rewards for moralists or idealists.

But The Law is fulfilled and the Beatifications prove true in a man, over whom the gods have lost their sway, and who, whilst staying in the fields of bondage, is not guided by their centrifugal forces but steadily faces the spaceless Center.

Who took up his Cross and gradually was "exalted," the helpless, languishing[10] one, who was helped by God (Eleasar, Lazarus, God helps), who "died" in the world of opposites, with Martha (Virgo) to his left, and Mary (Pisces) to his right, but is raised from the dead, as he enters The Open Field, which is "open" because there is neither Space nor Time. Who experienced in that Open Field a new consciousness, that made all things "new," for *recognized* in their *eternal* meaning, because he that has returned to the Source in this manner is being fed by the fruit of the Tree of Life.

*

The Kingdom of Heaven, that is the Holy Jerusalem, indeed has Twelve Gates (Rev.21), the Twelve bars of the Three Crosses, each of which bears the name of a Tribe of Israel. That is the Zodiac.

But the Foundation is formed by the Twelve of The Lamb, which symbolize the twelve-fold aspect of "Following the Master." This is the Sacred Zodiac, the Zodiac in its reversed sense.

For the Process of Liberation is not effected by any method of neglecting the Help offered by the Cosmic rhythm, but it works by the response of the individual to the specific possi-

---

[10] Greek: asthenoon!, that does not necessarily mean ïll,"but suffering, languishing."

bility which enables each of us to free himself of existing ties and to rise to a higher cadence of existence.

This possibility is hidden for us in what is offered to us every day as a Key that is handed to us again and again, so the person who is *turning himself around* can unlock one of the Gates of the Holy Zodiac.

Not in grandiosely successful expression of the character types of the twelve signs of the zodiac will the Twelve Labors of Hercules be accomplished, but in rising above the restrictions of the twelve types by conclusive response in Reversion to each of the twelve.

For all Twelve Gates, *as long as we pass through in reverse direction,* give access to the Holy Jerusalem.

The jewel of the Messianic Mystery lies in what is offered to us every day.

The confrontation with that is always concerned with abstinence from left and right, with response in the holy sense.

While we, fully caught up in our evaluation in contrasts, either pull the cord which lifts the "veil" or that which brings it down, not understanding that every effort of this kind is always perfectly compensated by a corresponding counter-effort, the waiting is for our pulling the Third Cord by which the Veil is torn and perishes.

But nobody can discern this Third Cord and pull it, until he has fully given up the endless game of Pro and Con, doing what the world despises and accepting what, in the eyes of the world, is death and destruction.

Not he who is prospering in the pairs of opposites, famous and honored, powerful and rich as a successful person, pleasing to God, and satisfies himself with the binding laws of nature, but he who, in want and losing, generally condemned and "Defeated" by the earthly powers escaping the charm and the grip of the "gods" to the final end by accepting time and again the Golden Key from God's Hand, will let himself be transformed by GOD into imperishability and will be able to say:

ALL IS FULFILLED.

This is how we can free events and circumstances from the essentially wrong cliché-judgment, which in its seemingly loving sympathy and pity robs our "fate" of its sacred familiarity and undermines our natural preference for it to any "normal" or "favorable" image of successful life. Instead of yielding to any system of compensation and equalization, as if our tasks were identical and equal in form, we shall turn anew in confidence to that strangely handicapped set of conditions which is our own in spite of all the disappointment and sorrow it has caused us. For we shall recognize in it a secret between God and ourselves, inaccessible to others; a secret which thanks to His Attention and our acceptance will be transformed into the narrow Gate, through which we shall return to Him as the seemingly neglected, seemingly lost Child.

The German poet Werner Bergengrün is right when he says:
-"Was dem Herzen sich verwehrte,
lass es schwinden unbewegt.
Allenthalben das Entbehrte
wird dir mystisch zugelegt."[11]

When the focus of our attention is indeed transferred from the enticing fields of the gods towards the Center of the Garden, where we are expected, then we will have left the cradle which the human race has been so fond of, the restrictions of which have been held on to so excessively, and which we perpetuate. Then we are "elevated." That is the Way of the Cross.

When this happens that mystical struggle called the Twilight of the Gods will be raised in us. It is the "dusk" that is as individual as those "Last Temptations" (or Final Things) of which the Gospel speaks. Both describe symbolically the divine Process, which attends and effects man's farewell to servitude and his Resurrection to Life Eternal.

In this seeming ruin this seemingly permanent consciousness of ours will prove merely a transitional stage, introduced by the unique response of some ancient forefather to the unique configuration which offered this exit from a preceding state of consciousness.

---

[11] What the heart denied itself, leave it to die off quietly. Everywhere you will mystically receive what was missing.

At last we shall drop the short-sighted idea that this consciousness of ours represents the highest possible realization of life, that man as he is today is the highest living form ever to develop.

And it will dawn upon us that what GOD is waiting for and expecting from us, is exactly this "laying down of our life of our own accord" that we may serve His Purpose in "taking up" Life of a higher kind, which HE has in store for us.

Then we shall no longer devote ourselves to vain efforts to perpetuate this present human race, but we shall know that our true vocation is to out-soar our present characterizing restrictions and so serve to usher in a nobler and happier race.

Acquiring this *new* understanding of Jesus' Message, we shall develop the inner discretion and confidence to give up the aggressive religious and idealistic striving to establish some preconceived "form" of individual and social life, and entrust ourselves to the Hands of Him, who alone can lead us to the state HE has prepared for us.

In that way, and that way only man can "give up his life to accept it anew." (John 10:17-18). Man has the power to do this out of his own free will and there is nothing for which God loves man as much as for this deed of love. But veiled unwillingness has also prevented this following of Jesus, by declaring it a monopoly of Jesus and thus to represent it as an unprecedented arrogance of "normal" people, to want to do this also. It is the old crime of the Pharisees, not to go in themselves and to also prohibit others from doing so.

Our natural tendency is not to give up our life willingly, but to keep it... and thereby to lose it. For this preservation effort no price is too high, even if it means someone else's life. That is why we who want to keep it that way will lose it.

But losing our life for the sake of the sanctification that Jesus consummated, we will accept it "new." For then we will be "elevated."

Then we shall no longer expect fulfillment from forming and reforming, image-worship and image-breaking, and in consequence thereof our life will lose the repetitive element caused by dealing with phenomena as if they were mere classifiable forms instead of unique meanings embodied in their disguise.

Then our existence will assume a genuinely eschatological character, which should not be misunderstood as the effect of foreknowledge of some tragic death, either by the hand of the world or as the result of mental disintegration, but as *the mark of response* to the *essence* of things, thus of recognition of the golden thread in all situations and the true "reckoning" with everything that is to be Done therein - and this Reckoning is, of course, final and unique.

Then we shall no longer live our part in this transition as down-hearted, faintly resisting "victims" and then we shall no longer take part in the arrogant tactics of the powerful of the earth to abuse the people with cleverness and force to continue present forms of society, which long ago have proved to be either "leftist" or "rightist" systems of exploitation; equally we will not participate in the hateful destruction or forceful imposition of any other system of human making.

But we shall have turned our soul's face to the Center, shunned by left and right alike, and we shall tread paths, where we meet fellow men neither as "enemies" (because of contrary interests), nor as "comrades" (because of similar interests), but as free Children of GOD, who, without coercion, without so-called discipline (which is only a mask of cruelty and perversion), without the hypocrisy, the hatred and retaliation which form-dictatorship instigates, approach each other full of goodwill and readily COOPERATING in the revelation of GOD'S WILL; not as an improvement to the sublunar order, but as a Departure from there into the Kingdom that is not of this world.

For "the world" is the world, and however more beautiful she is made out to be by representations from those in power and with "authority," that much more misleading she will be, since she serves the "talking Snake."

Never can her institutions house the unconditional Love, with which the few followers of Jesus love each other and... by which they can be recognized. (John 13:34-35).

But in the midst of this "world" we will discover the Holy Way, that leads to the One Goal; which Isaiah foresaw (Is. 35:4-10) and which Jesus taught... and went. The Way which he IS!

This lonely Way towards Brotherhood, is the Way to the Open Field. Again some few will go this Way, and once more the blind will receive their sight and the lame will walk, lepers will be cleansed and the deaf will hear, the "dead" will be raised up and the dejected will receive good news; for once more the Living Water will flow in "the desert."

Few will be the first flowers in the Garden of Eden.

But also the many who once again do not follow, will gain strength for the future from this "revelation of God's Works" by reason of the certainty that it is not all pointless and in vain, because the dethronement of human images of GOD will have opened the receptiveness for the *experience that He exists and rules His creation, but that He will always be "who He will be," giving while he takes and taking while he gives (=Joseph, related to asaph and jasaph), in His Rule which is unassailable for human arrogance and rebellion.*

THE END

Birth Pangs of New Man

World crisis and heavenly plan

The complexity of conscious human life is exceeded by the complexities of the human body. Whoever looks for structure in it is always overwhelmed by relationships and correlations that seem fundamental but nevertheless are not. Out of that a fragmentary vision arises a piece of theory, because the one-sided logical connection always appears to encompass the whole. But those are all "floating islands" of orientation, local areas of temporarily successful reassurance. One feels strengthened by them in facing "life" and especially also those fellow men, who, in their turn, possess one or more islands of "certainty" about the unknowable and who, from that position, sound out their "truth" so disappointingly for us and so triumphantly for themselves and shed their "light" on our nebulous condition.

Exact science has attempted to prevent this lack of a basis by starting from an axiom. Since the axiom proves not to be the basis, from time to time strange revisions, compromises, or an apparent widening of the horizon are necessary (astronomy, electricity, theory of light, theory of relativity, etc.).

The "insular" character and the "floating" nature show themselves sooner or later. Philosophy and the spiritual sciences have the character of floating islands in the unmanageable oceanic reality right from the outset.

Hence the fact that the specialists are always noticeably "king" of a limited territory and always have to feel threatened in their position by the position of other "kings" and therefore sooner or later come to blows with those other "kings." When that happens, hordes of vassals (would-be kings) participate in the more or less organized battle. The significant fact about this (as about any other) battle is that none of the parties is above the battle, that none of the parties truly uses the battle as a means, but that the battle happens to them. Neither beginning, nor end, nor course, nor outcome of the battle is in the hands of the combatants. Parenthetically, this throws a curious light on war and war preparation, on diplomacy and politics.

But philosophically it all is more subtle and more veiled in its very aggressiveness. Philosophically, nearly everything and everyone approaches the world or another person with an air of peace and peace loving. The striving may be ever so much for peace but in the wrong way, and already the forced withholding of the one and advancing of the other lead to an unrealistic present of "as if," that never *can* be the Way to Peace. The Way of Heaven evokes all wretchedness, everything that could be in the way of Peace; it calls all that had been artfully and carefully hidden and concealed into the foreground, so it shows itself and acts itself out, and thereby shows its lack of validity to itself.

Meetings of philosophies about life can never be anything else but a tournament of island-kings, a tournament that all too easily degenerates into an embittered battle. For the misguided intention of supremacy is innate in all those kings. That delusion is in wanting to be and having to be "king." The forever unseen Free person, the intrinsically successful and happy person, who found Peace, can never be "king" in any way whatsoever unless it be of a Kingdom that "is not of this earth."

We can feel strange when we realize that we meet one another in our philosophies of life and therefore not directly; that we exchange our preliminary orientation which, because of its very insufficiency, makes us prepared to seek contact with other orientations. Conviction, after all, usurps the place of Insight and realization! It is all armor and arsenal and serves only the battle that should not be! Because, in truth, there is nothing to fight for but to Be and from that Being, to Do.

Equally strange is it that human brains attempt to take control when they do not know enough and cannot handle it, that human brains are dull and slow compared to the unequaled organisms of the living bodies, and that we continually set out in life to work with living beings in a grossly inadequate manner, more or less like plundering barbarians in the temples of a past culture.

A lot of knowledge about the periphery, much understanding of the values and forms in the periphery, lend a certain potency with respect to phenomena in the periphery but force man to limit and confine himself to what is peculiar to the periphery. The observing of and working with the peculiarities of the periphery gradually enclose the awareness in the sphere of the periphery. Gradually there seems to be no more reason, no more desirability for that particular human being to turn away from the periphery, and thus to turn to the center.

The lives of famous people who concentrated on the periphery have always demonstrated this. At the same time, their life histories showed mostly (despite themselves) a getting lost in, being confronted with, or being overwhelmed by the center, the life-long-denied-central theme, the absolutely unknowable and unfathomable.

This can be seen relatively easily in the lives of the imperious (monarchs, dictators, conquerors, etc.) and of scientists. Sometimes it can also be seen in the lives of great artists. Sooner or later they came into a position in which their power turned into powerlessness, their knowledge to unknowing, their insight into consternation, their fame to rejection, their glorification of the external to veneration of the inner, the abstract, their feeling of fathoming to awareness of the unfathomable.

With much more difficulty, the same liberating course of events can be discerned in the philosophies of life. But precisely because the philosophies of life as "systems" are the pseudo-following of unique accomplishment, the systems must lead to a crisis, if applied long enough to the reality of life, confronting the person with the incomparable reality of his unfathomable life task, which he has attempted for so long to realize with a mass produced opinion, and which he has only made unreal.

Therefore, this is what really happens in the meeting of philosophies of life, that people impress each other with their limited sovereign powers and at the same time catch one another at their distortions of life.

It is really naive to expect that truth could ever spring from a "clash of opinions." The barrenness of discussion is in the fact that the faintly intended, but difficult to express, deeper and deepest values are flatly replaced with deductions and conclusions of the logical context. As in a debate the most eloquent wins the "battle," likewise in any discussion the conclusion goes where one-sided logical reasoning leads it. That can never be anything else but a strictly logical position, thus a crass one-sided denial of the unfathomable essence of Life.

Therefore, it would be madness to invite people to release their attitudes about life and their life philosophies on one another as if in a tournament, if it were not that each of the participants consciously or unconsciously has the hankering and the preparedness to assimilate something "else" besides what the other participants can offer him, namely something of the Truth itself. Where people come together with this hankering and barely conscious or completely unconscious preparedness to meet and receive the uninvited, or even unwanted, there God's Holy Spirit finds the occasion to sow in that hankering His Seed of Truth and Life, in the midst of human exchange of thoughts and their tournament of opinions.

This way the word from the Gospel is fulfilled already: "Where two or three are together in my 'name,' there I am in their midst."

It is oppressive to think how little we do justice to this truth in meetings with others. The Effect will, of course, never be a correction to the conviction of this or that person. It will always be the unmasking of a motive, a position becoming untenable, the tarnishing of an idol. It is as if GOD Himself rummages around in the packaging of our ballast, and the fake jewels roll onto the floor, as if He Himself blows the pseudo-crown from our unenlightened heads. Then we feel shortchanged, grieved, or upset.

The truth is that our brain and its understanding are only clumsy and undifferentiated tools for observing the purposefulness of what eon after eon has responded to the laws of nature, makes nature a Study book for all who prefer truth to the preliminary ready wit of a "philosophy of life."

In lieu of the Study book of Nature, most people still prefer a "study book about nature," thus replacing the revealed true reality with an analytical, deterministic mental product *about* nature, in which human powerlessness, wretchedness, and life philosophy are built in.

Thus we experience and continually eat and drink each others' misformation and the products of our own misformation and thus hope to approach the true and beautiful. What else is human intercourse but to charm and be charmed by each others' wretchedness, to gradually (in an endless string of disappointments) arrive at the awareness that behind the represented and initially accepted things the true reality, the true Face, the truly beautiful Figure, the One Beloved One, GOD HIMSELF, is present and beckons, beckons...

* *

The Study book of Nature is Present and Past in one, not as truth, but as reality, as response to Truth: response to the confrontation of essence and order in a consistent implementation which far transcends our understanding.

In its innumerable pluriformity of appearances in the periphery, the original foundation, as the root of all that is, has risen up in its implementation and in this expression of itself; it is almost hidden in that expression.

Nevertheless, it is not renounced or destroyed, just as the roots of a tree are not renounced or destroyed by the trunk, branches, and leaves. Time and space were the possibility and the task at the same time.

Descending in time alone will therefore not lead to observation of the fundamental, the primary. The combination of time and space alone contains the meaning of essence-revealing in creation, revelation of the essence that is neither of time nor of space, but timeless and spaceless.

If creation stands opposite to the Creator, life in creation is as that which Is with-GOD, as the God-connected and divine, God-revealing, opposite to creation, as essence in the opportunity to reveal essence.

Life itself, therefore, is timeless/spaceless, essential, like GOD.

The forms that life takes to manifest itself therefore at the same time reveal GOD in His creation. The non-living in creation is matter as maternal substance in which GOD creates life. That is the reason that living matter manifests the essence (the nature) of GOD in the nature of matter .

Living matter thus promptly begins to differentiate itself from dead matter, and the difference that is manifested in this way is fundamental for the expression of life.

If for dead matter there is no other "existence" in time and space than the greatest possible resistance in inevitably being changed, living matter "exists" by continual change of itself, that is to say, life triumphs over the impotence of matter against time and space. Life is not something passive that takes its power from inertia, but something active, that shows its power from moment to moment because it does not maintain its form, but maintains itself in the spatial and temporal order by continual replacement of that form.

That is to say that, as opposed to the pseudo-persistence of matter, which, in reality, is a slowed down perishing, life poses a Persistence *without* the rigidity of living form, but with a renewal of form which is as perfect as possible.

This moving victory over the rigor of death as "being resistant" against spatial/temporal being as Standing up in maintenance of essence in self-wrought renewal of form is the primary *deed* of life, the most fundamental Living-deed, which Nature presents to us in billion fold applications, specializations, and analogies.

As a symbol of an innumerable number of forms, this essence of Life manifests itself in the nature of the plant kingdom, the animal kingdom, and the human realm.

Standing up and *holding up* are symbolized in space in the vertical, in the pillar, in whatever bears up in silence and stands upright. It is the arch-expression of life as holy will and takes on the air of a connecting line between Creator and creation, between GOD and creature, for it expresses itself not only en masse, but individually as well.

This arch quality of life[1], standing up as erection from the plane of lifelessness, is depicted in the plant kingdom in a dignity and faithfulness which often put to shame the corresponding expression in "higher" beings.

The way a flower-bearing plant stalk moves us, or the way a very straight giant pine or poplar impresses us, or the dignity of a fully developed oak or beech tree - they are not anthropomorphic misinterpretations by man, who forever projects himself into everything. But it is the *meeting and recognizing* of the same arch quality of life in forms of expression of life totally different from the human one, a beginning of experiencing the recognition of the Unity of all Life.

This standing up is the arch principle of all holding steady in faithfulness to life, also in man and his bodily erectness, as well as in his uprightness of inner being, his "standing up" in

---

[1] These three principles were described earlier by Valentin Tomberg in *Die Vier Christus-opfer*, where he unfortunately treats them in a strange doctrinaire fashion, and interprets them pathetically.

the midst of the forces that pull him down, his faithfulness to God in creation.

It makes man into the vertical one, a pillar, into the bearer of the Wood, the pillory to which he is tied because of his faithfulness in the material world, and because "the world," that which has yielded to the way of death, has to hate him. For his appearance reminds them of their own task and failing. But it makes man into a representation of the Tree of Life, the first transubstantiation of the living soul into the life-giving spirit!

Another arch quality of life is that it does not exist in isolation, but in experience of connectedness with GOD in a relationship of devoted attention, and even extends that attention to lifeless matter.

It stands up in the unity of life and in the unity of all that has been created although the separateness of the living forms and the discord among those forms, as well as the disfavor of the lifeless forms, bring about an experience of utter Loneliness which becomes worse as the warm attentiveness manifests itself in the living form.

The manifestation of this arch quality occurs again from the lowest to the highest forms of life, in plant and animal kingdoms, and in the human realm not only in those levels that man shares with the animals, but also in the typically human relationship to the abstract.

And with this, man fulfills his "having been created in GOD's image," in that he *gives attention* to all that is, empathizes with all that lives as much as possible, and feels with and is able to express himself in more than primitive sharing and commonness even in commiseration and compassion, taking pity in GOD's Name on life in need.

This is the living Horizontal, which expresses the connectedness in its broadest sense, and as a Symbol, it is the Horizontal of the Cross, on which the Son of Man willingly goes and gives himself, taking pity on all that lives as Lord of Compassion, in the bondage of all Life bound to time and space... and thus to GOD.

It is the victory of Loneliness because no separation and separateness can overcome the essential connectedness.

There is a third arch quality which manifests itself in the plant kingdom as receptiveness for impressions and reaction to them in order to guard life or as adaptation to circumstances, as response to what is happening and what forms those circumstances, which seemingly dictate the living *conditions*. Seemingly, for Life creates its own fulfillment of conditions. It carries within itself the Memory of the truly conditional, the Memory of What Is in the midst of what appears to be, which forces itself upon us as What Is.

Only the relativizing of all circumstances, all impressions that the living being experiences, lets it be faithful to What Is. The defense that all plants, animals, and people show against the aggressiveness of the impressions, which are the inevitable consequence of their horizontal attention and receptiveness, takes place out of Remembrance and Faith to the essential self.

In the animal kingdom we call this ability instinct; in man we speak of intuition and conscience as aids in understanding what escapes us. For intuition cannot be grasped by the intellect, and conscience varies from mass-trained behavior to the "conscience of the soul," as unfathomable as intuition.

That is exactly why our abstract usage of sensual perception is so revealing: seeing for understanding, hearing for recognizing, feeling for realizing, tasting and also smelling for perceiving. Hearing and Seeing are not independent of each other, but rather presuppose each other, the one protecting us from the charming power of the other. Deeper, closer to the essence is Hearing as compared with Seeing. Visual impressions are more external than audible impressions, which in themselves are understood as "expression" of something internal.

Seeing reaches to the "following" of spiritual development in external appearance. Hearing finds its fullness in Understanding.

We find the highest expression of Remembrance in the remembrance of the Father by the Prodigal Son, the remembrance of the Creator by the creature, the "looking after" creation by GOD. "Do this for my remembrance."

It is the triumph of What Is over nearly overwhelming appearances. It is the ability to forget all the incidentals for the sake of being mindful of The One Necessity.

* *

The inner history of mankind is the path of becoming human. It is the development of the manifestation of life from the animal level to the full realization of the gradually available possibilities, through which true man gradually emerges.

We, who are under way, do not know the true Man, the Son of Man. We have a concept of the full realization of being-human, a concept that has been determined by our subjective and massively impure attitude of feeling and thinking. We have an affect-laden mental *image* in which inevitably our mass and individual tendencies have free play. As much as we "see" the present and ourselves in the present with that deviation from reality which corresponds with our mutilating and coloring perception, we misunderstand True Man in our conception of him. We can only idealize ourselves. Therefore we can strive for the realization of true Man as little as for our own unknown individual Destiny. We all strive - as long as we strive - for the realization of our ideal, even though we gradually realize that our ideal is not real, that we can never reach it because it is no more than a reflection which changes as we proceed.

It can be understood that our backward outlook will not be free of mystification, even when that outlook imagines itself to be confirmed in all kinds of detail findings of past appearances of the periphery.

Even scientific research does not escape that, for it is the interpretation of and conclusion from the exact facts which introduces a factor of misunderstanding.

But the arch qualities of life are unshakably valid from the beginning till now and will be valid until the end of time. They manifested themselves by the long development path that is behind us and will manifest themselves until we have reached our Destination.

They are the absolutely reliable lights in the night of unknowing of our soul, the light beacons that determine our route where we are unable to chart our course over the abysmal waters of the mystery of life.

THEREFORE, WE WILL BE ABLE AT ALL TIMES TO OBSERVE OUR DEVIATION FROM THE ONE TRUE COURSE IN OUR NEGATIONS AND DENIAL OF THE ARCH QUALITIES AND BE ABLE TO CHANGE THE ATTITUDE OF OUR SOUL CORRESPONDINGLY.

So that we do not go *under* by the denial of the essence of life.

The question whether our life attitude and life deeds **now** express the arch qualities of life faithfully is **the** Question of Conscience for humanity as a whole and for every individual.

Do we stand up as a manifestation of our timeless being in the midst of the transience of time and space?

Do we stand up like a pillar directed towards heaven in the midst of the down-dragging, leveling forces of pseudo-life which are forces of death?

Do we bear what flowers in us like a plant stalk in moving erectness? Do we bear the resistance against this erectness with the dignity of a tree?

Does our collective and individual presence and activity in the world have the true gesture of all encompassing well-disposed connectedness?

Are we our brothers' keepers?

Or are we collectively and individually "lonely" in dejected, introverted self-glorification and, consequently, still proceeding with the life-denying repetition of the tragedy of Cain and Abel?

Are our life attitude and our life development a manifestation of the triumph of life over the circumstances, the supremacy of the essence over the forms in which it expresses itself?

Or do we demonstrate grandiosely that we consider life dependent on conditions and forms, always using those as fixed starting points of our conduct?

Do we aim fearlessly for the expression of our essence in the certainty that circumstances can only be possibilities to do so and never impediments? Or is our entire collective and individual existence these days aimed at the creation of "favorable" conditions in the delusion that these will then determine what life expression will come crawling out of our soul-less essence?

The answer to these questions of conscience is the unrelenting Judgment of our well-established, mutually-sanctioned DE-NIAL OF LIFE, which, nonetheless, cries out to the heavens above.

Do we not recognize the arch qualities?

Is it not these essential characteristics of life which compelled all true experience of God's will to Commandments, to a Law of Life, to quiet praise to Tao, to the Mystery reflections of the Near East, to speculations concerning the so-called double Order of Life and Death in the so-called Egyptian Book of the Dead (which in reality is called "Exit to the Light"), to the teachings of the Mahabharata and of Gautama the Enlightened, to the teachings of the man of Nazareth and his Achievement?

Do we not recognize with a shock that the Jesus manifestation, choked and entangled in sweetness and moralistic poses by later generations, was the fulfillment of the Law of Life by a person before the eyes of a world that no longer "saw" exactly *that*?

Do we not recognize that behind his Teachings is his Accomplishment, not purely and only the accomplishment of a via dolorosa because of the hatred and denial of those who deny life, but precisely and primarily his actual faithfulness to the three arch marks of life?

To hold up in the seemingly endless Fasting imposed by GOD; to venture out into life with His seemingly too sparse, all-too-veiled Word.

While all around stones are made into bread and the world in its massive power, as well as our own innate tendency to yield, pressure us and force us to cooperate with this producing and eating of "a substitute which does not feed the soul."

To stand up in the temptation of letting humanity and its demands and promises become a motive and pseudo-justification for what is, in truth, prostitution to the infernal, the objectionable.

To stand up in the Remembrance of the essence of life: Servitude to GOD, amidst the general denial of this *singular* dependence, because people deem themselves dependent on one another, and one forces the other continually in the false relationship of Lord and Servant (employer and employee) in thousand fold variations, with the equally false promise: to give him power and possessions as pay for that betrayal of the essence of human relations.

We have neatly kept this threefold standing up, this one and only acte de présence of being human, outside of Jesus' teachings.

Not that we are true to the Sermon on the Mount; not that we "do according to the Word," "keep" Jesus' Word, as he called it! We have found another way of "keeping:" thousand fold translations and printing and distributing by means of propaganda as common in commerce and... with violence to back it up. For those who have yielded to a show of force are docile subjects.

But the accomplishment of the threefold Temptation, the actual accomplishment of faithfulness to the essence of Life, we have neatly reduced to hors d'oeuvres.

We do not think of "following after him" in that sense. After all, we do not follow him at all and always find a way out by deifying him and his "vicarious suffering."

Many millions have recognized him and acknowledged him as the Accomplisher; many millions confess to him in theory, be it as a historical appearance, be it as a highest ideal.

A relatively small number of millions reject him in theory and practice on the basis of contrary orientation, a reaction to those who propagated him and his teachings, but in fact denied him and his teachings.

The split mind of the pseudo-Christians shows in their acknowledging him, but *in fact* rejecting his Teachings in their actual life.

It has truly not gone in favor of his meaning and intentions. It is as if a fierce contrary interference started at his appearance and continued after his disappearance.

Nevertheless, his Words do not perish; in accordance with God's Will they offered the possibility of a higher level of life for people and were their "Salvation" by an exemplary fundamental victory over exactly those predestinations to yielding which, in the era that is now completed, almost universally brought man to a far advanced denial of the three arch qualities, a far advanced failing in the three temptations which Jesus withstood.

The collective Image that humanity exhibits, is *not* the image of the Follower of Jesus Christ, but the image of the Antichrist!

While we expect him to be the umpteenth tyrant, for whom we blindly and unresistingly kneel down, he has manifested himself million fold, almost invincibly in the average man, who chooses the "shepherd" that he deserves.

Not capitalism, democracy, or fascism, or Marxism, not one group or another, be it political or religious or non-religious, threaten the existence of mankind, similarly not nuclear bombs, or nuclear physics and radioactivity.

The self-induced blindness of people makes them ascribe the power of destruction of humanity to this or that ruler, to this or that deed of human irresponsibility.

All of this reduces reality without insight to the deluded positions of prejudiced groups.

The big Threat for the average man of today is the Keeper of peoples!

Threat, because the authority of the arch qualities posed by Him have been replaced to an absurd extent by the pseudo authority of pseudo-experts and pseudo-shepherds.

For even if the uprising of the masses may be signaled in a certain facet of human relations, the True and essential Uprising which has taken shape over the centuries is THE UPRISING OF HUMANITY AGAINST GOD.

Its leaders, worldly and spiritual, are included in that because they are leaders only on the basis of their complicity.

This is the true Uprising, and attention to facets of it diverts attention from the general, essential phenomenon.

This Uprising came into being by the consistent continuation of denial of the three arch qualities. And we would perish from this continuation if Jesus, fulfilling his calling, had not in principle conquered this all-too-human rebelliousness by his life; if he had not already then given the Answer which protects and delivers, if he had not already then given the Teachings which CURE this monstrous illness, this degenerating inclination... if only it were accepted and really applied.

Our half-conscious betrayal of life causes ever greater fear. Our *eating of stones* causes us to be ever more dissatisfied, causes hankering and determined striving for life extension because the years go by in deprivation of life, and death seems all the more tragic. Our boundless freebootery in so-called self-determination increases sorrows and problems to an unbearable degree and makes us into pseudo-meritorious haulers of a needless, pointless load (Atlas!). And our continual pseudo service of human authority and human power for the sake of the promised wages as possessions, safety, and power, has made us into dissatisfied *slaves* who demand and expect from human beings what GOD *alone* gives to His Servant.

Because it cannot go on like this any longer, because the general dissatisfaction has become a constant need, the problems have become a constant crisis, and the power balances have been increased to madness so that they bind the central activities and the central attention of people, therefore the Almighty intervenes and responds to the human show of power with imposition of experience of powerlessness, which cures their power madness.

Because we have used power to excess and directly and indirectly have played Cain's role for a long time, HE will put us in the defenselessness of Abel until we are cured of our belief in violence.

Because we have replaced the response from the heart with legal obligations, voluntary helpfulness and voluntary service with rigidly formulated, forced duty, the simply "evil" will take on the form of duty till we are cured of the tendency to obtain by force whatever is not given in love.

And the unsatisfying stones which we bake for ourselves and our fellow human beings will make us so empty inside that we will loathe the substitute that was offered and swallowed so excessively. We will Fast in the deprivation imposed by GOD rather than to let ourselves be stuffed any longer with the poisonous, sweet pseudo-food.

When we are confronted with the consequences of wrong responses to what is offered, which have been implemented for a long time, then an observed causal connection will appear to our analytical deterministic brain to be all we are looking for, whereas it can, of course, never be more than a fragment, which is understood in that manner in its right to exist. Then we speak of removing a cause, as if the observed phenomena indeed existed in isolation, that it could be rectified or nullified.

This is really "doctoring," unconsciously, humorously chosen as a word for the common human interference in many areas, derived from the sort of medical assistance that did not in any way rest on diagnosis in the true sense of the word. Man lacks dia-gnosis.[2]

Thus it is understandable that, regarding the upsetting degeneration in mankind, we understand that deterioration much too narrowly in a much too limited way with our notion

[2]The meaning of the Greek word diagnosis is: seeing through.

of causality, much too much tied to certain areas of the philosophy of life and life attitude.

This leads to one-sided "explaining" and one-sided "striving" for improvement, and people go to work politically, economically, moralistically, humanistically, religiously, or any other way, without realizing that these very institutions prove by themselves that man never responds with his full humanity to the fullness of what is offered, but always with specialized attention and specialized orientation.

It is no wonder that our "doctoring" always fails, because it turns its attention and involvement away from the whole as much as it concentrates on the fragment.

In a time of crisis like the present one, we therefore see the purposeful and accidental "specialists" put themselves forward as experts and reorganizers of it all.

But humanity is like that woman who suffered bleedings for twelve years, "and had suffered many things of many physicians, and had spent all that she had, and was nothing bettered, but rather grew worse" (Mark 5:25-26).

Just because the need is so great, humanity will intuitively, just like that woman in her need, touch the garment in which God's Salvation manifests himself ...

* *

The cause of our need is not hidden or tucked away, but lies deeper than our nearsighted specialist eyes look.

It is in our human development, in our failure to commit ourselves continuously and fully to life. It is *life*-need. For human development demands long lasting and continual commitment to life in the, at first, seemingly overpowering order of what is lifeless in nature. The development of Life itself generates life, bringing to life all that is dead. And becoming human is a phase in that development. Becoming human is a continuation of what was accomplished in the plant and animal kingdoms *by arising from the limitations of those areas of life.*

This can be achieved *only* by a fuller, higher commitment to Life in the midst of the always oppressive claims of the order of the lifeless *and* of the claims of a past status of life.

On this long pilgrimage the three arch qualities of life have undiminished validity as the criteria of accomplishment or failure. Every momentary individual accomplishment lifts up the deadly circle of repetition, changes the development along that circle into a course along a rising spiral. At the same time, this elevation means a widening, a new possibility because of a widened consciousness *and* a new possibility for failure in the response to what is new.

Historically, it most likely developed so that relatively long phases of circulation at a certain level led to "tension," because the urge for life could not countenance a partial denial of life and this need would then have led to an initiative. An initiative which was not just an adventure, but inevitably had the meaning of a Sacrifice - a sacrifice of whatever was "best" until now, to make room for the unknown "better."

This living truth sounds like religion, because Life *is* Service to God.

The *root* of our present "failure" in the realization of Life, thus lies in the wanting response in the "transitions." For it is clear, that the shortfall in our response during the phases that are behind us ill prepares us, if not makes us unable to make the Sacrifice that is demanded silently at the time of a Transition to a higher, richer level of life.

Precisely because such a Transition to a higher level of life is happening **now** and it finds us hardly prepared, hardly at all able to make the Sacrifice, we may be thankful that at least *one* fundamental Memento exists, one orientation mark in the history of development of life on earth: the recognizable registration of the essential occurrence of all times.

When we arrive at an indication of this occurrence in the past, then this will not satisfy the demands of an exact or inexact scientific approach, nor those of philosophy or religious speculation. This would be madness anyway because *our* purpose is *not* a deliberately limited consciousness but precisely a growing awareness, as unlimited as possible, of what is essential. The following indications are therefore neither exact nor unimpeachable. They are indications, that is to say, they do not pretend to be the truth (which is what products of thinking always do!), but they point to the truth. The truth that does not *let* itself be said.

Living matter has consciousness, becomes aware of itself. On the long road from matter to spirit, which cancels the opposition between the two by *bridging* it, the centralization of life develops self-knowledge, awareness of itself in given restrictions and therefore not only self-awareness but ultimately all-awareness. Always in opposites, in which the truth only manifests itself as a paradox. Does form bear life, or does life bear form? Our questions arise from our own split into opposites. In all valuation, the truth is the silent third, which cannot be said but which is the only one that exists and decides.

In response to the arch qualities, the living cells devote themselves to a task that differentiates itself, and the different parts of living organisms have their own task and task awareness which is in a harmonious relationship with the other centers of awareness. Thus organs develop which function in a rapport with one another. Metabolism forces assimilation of food, and secretion of decay, breathing, circulation, and conduction of reactions, gradually, to the central nervous system and the brain. What comes, comes *only* through transgression of what exists as magical *self*-surpassing, as creation of new form by life.

In spite of all appearances, Life never kills itself but it vanquishes form after form and thus breaks the stagnation of the temporary fruit of Life.

Only the attachment to form in us, our own inner stagnation, makes us see the course of nature as a display of self destructive life and leads us to aversion, indignation, and ... one-sided interference.

It is not accidental that the first arch quality manifests itself so strikingly in plants, the second so strikingly in animals, and the third primarily in the human realm. It is as if the successive waves of possibility of manifestation developed a response, without the previous one being less intrinsic, less fundamental. On the contrary, at the same time the previous arch quality manifested itself in a higher fashion, on a higher, more abstract level.

The human skeleton fulfills the bearing uprightness once again, but now in cohesion with the inner uprightness, uprightness of soul, turning towards God.

It symbolizes not only the vertical of the Cross as sacrificial path, but above all the Resurrection itself, because it elevates itself from the plane from which it arose.

In its unshakable condition of attraction and repulsion for the sake of the manifestation of life, it lends a self-centeredness, the ability to defend itself in every respect by determining and keeping distance.

In its highest dignity it serves as a basis when a new Figure, that no longer is of this earth, is shaped by GOD.

The horizontal attention (with whatever intention) found its possibility and expression in the freedom to move, which separates the animal from the plant, movement in many variations, mostly unequaled in grace, always with interest, which can be purified to the attention and devotion of the animal.

In man, it manifests itself bodily as well as spiritually, with the emphasis on the latter; it manifests itself at an unquestionably higher level, and combined with a mindfulness which lifts the attention above the limitations of the external actuality and activates past and future-expectation, and at the same time as a preparatory stage of human attention, prepared from Above, which elevates itself above time and space and in due course directs itself to God's Attention for man.

All consciousness presupposes more than the field of consciousness alone. Consciousness, also cellular consciousness, is a "rapport" with something that is less peripheral, less manifest, more central, more causal.

Living organisms do not exist without a complimentary "double" which, as an indispensable background, maintains the balance which would be disturbed by one sided physical manifestation.

Conscious denial and unconscious betrayal of this "rapport" cause languishing life, degeneration of cells and organ functions, in other words disease.

Spaceless, timeless Life which manifests itself in space and time does not allow itself to be halved into a bundle of one-sidedness in the pairs of opposites. With our visible *inside* there is an invisible *outside*, with our left a right, with our forwards a backwards, with every movement, with every impression, a compensating one in which our life here is registered.

This "rapport" can be called the very first form of "conscience," which by calling for faithfulness to life, arouses the first discord with the stagnating circulation in the order of lifeless matter.

Thus, it will have led to a need which turned into sacrifice of form, in order that life create a truer form. There is the first triumph of life, the manifestation of the first arch quality, standing up in uprightness.

But where this "rapport" weakens, the functions lose their healthy functionality. There, movements automatically become ungracious. There, organs will be misunderstood as mechanisms, there, the whole body is a machine.

This is what we see in a disconcerting degree in the attitude of people towards what their body is and needs. Our posture, although erect, seldom has the purity and dignity that a tree shows. We consider our body as a bothersome machine. We judge it under the influence of the rigid products of our thinking: the machine, guided by the characteristics of the machine. We feel we need an "overhaul," a fix-up, a partial replacement (artificial organs!). We make the doctor into a mechanic and demand that he become an accomplice, instead of furtherance of healing.

Thus, we fail more than plant and animal in our faithfulness to the first arch quality. And we stack failure upon failure, combining several in the different phases of development of consciousness.

Like a good tree puts us to shame in our failing uprightness, and plants and animals put us to shame with their simple faithfulness to the "rapport" with their unseen "double," thus the animal puts us to shame on a grand scale by its gracious movement, where we go around on earth cumbersomely, slowly, awkwardly.

The few exceptions, of course, confirm the rule.

But the second arch quality offers unendingly more opportunities for accomplishing and failing.

Releasing movement after the motionlessness of the plant kingdom created an enormous realm of relationships for living beings among each other (senses, voice).

Movement liberated them from the isolation of a solitary existence, it liberated the living being from *Loneliness*. The pairs of opposites urged to sympathy and antipathy. Consciousness expanded from feeding-, growth-, and metabolic process, to meeting-connecting-solidarity, fulfilling desires in exchange etc.; in short, the consciousness of life received a new domain, a less physical realm, the realm of what we call emotional life.

And small wonder that the newly-opened realm became the center or point of gravity of consciousness even if we still see a lot of emphasis on the life processes in animals.

The newly opened realm opened temptation to swooning in sensations, swooning in you-and-I as a prototype of what is still notably important in human relations, up to a cult of idylls, a cult of beauty in the human realm.

The anchoring of the self in these things leads to the abuse of fellow human beings, and of relationships to fellow human beings; it leads to abuse and force, parasitism, and throwing away of oneself (narcotics).

"If you are God's Son, cast yourself down ..."

Much, much later, the power of reasoning had been developed and with it the ego-consciousness. For thinking has a thinker, and this thinker therefore evermore realizes his own existence as a center.

The emphasis of consciousness now of course shifted to this newly opened realm, the realm of thought. The one who came last easily mistakes himself for the last one who *could* come, therefore the highest and best. And will therefore be the least prepared to make room in turn for... what comes *then*.

The evolving "ego" - it has sometimes been said that this "ego" consciousness was only really established just before the Christian era - can not help it that it deems itself a center, that it feels called upon - even though it is a *form - to maintain itself* and thus to deny Life!

But it feels "alone" in this pseudo-centrality and this loneliness causes the delusion of obligations and rights. *There is no "right" and there is no "obligation" but the delusions of the affect-laden products of the "ego's" thinking.* There is *only* Life that has been given which is in essence Servitude to GOD. This demands that we love it with all our soul, with all our heart, with all our emotions, and with all our power.

The rest is man-made, issued forth from denial and renouncing of life because of fear of life.

Especially this delusion of "being-left-alone" demonstrates the *Oblivion* of the true Center, of the All. Awareness of the microcosm seduced us to forgetting the macrocosm. Man, equipped with four types of consciousness (four bodies if you wish), decided for autonomy and independence except from his own ability, for non-existence of the Center, and non-existence of GOD.

That is where atheism has its roots. Not only in contrary orientation to repulsive pseudo-belief and pseudo God-cult but also in the delusions of the thinking "ego." Thinking can not liberate a person from that delusion. Thinking can not "know" itself. At best it "knows" its relativity without being able to apply this knowledge consistently.

This phase of our development has truly led to a degeneration of attitude and behavior of humanity.

In this phase it came to a combination of old forms of yielding, dating back to the previous phases of development. Complicated abuse of thinking led not only to fundamental overestimation of one's powers, which is characteristic of many forms of human deformity and in evident contradiction with itself as in for example: theology, moralism, intellectualism, materialism, anarchism, nihilism, etc., but perfidious thinking, ego-serving thinking, *joined forces* with unhappy emotions, desires, and urges in a convoluted degeneration of human relations in all areas of life. *"All this will I will give you, if you serve me."*

* *

Our so-called society is nothing but a complicated system of "rights and obligations," of rules for mutual exploitation. The "ego" is obsessed with power in the realm of life denial. *Therefore everything today strives for power.* Power as triumph, as victory over all other striving, as safety, as living space and opportunity to live.

But Life does not need any of this for it *is*, thanks to God's *Al*mightiness. Institutions of power, secular or religious, are therefore marked a priori as Life-denial and thus as revolt against God.

We have not only "betrayed" the first and second quality. We have not only replaced the movement given to us by pseudo movement, namely being moved: by bike, by train, by car, by plane, thereby once again forgetting our "rapport" and *causing the degeneration of our bodily functions.*

We have above all, continuing on with those denials, let our connection to God sink away into oblivion. With that we have denied and crippled human relationships and human existence, our true life goal, into a tragic parody.

And now that this phase is at an end, as a fullness of time, and now that Life calls us to Go up to a higher level of life, now that we are invited and forced to the Accomplishment of the upward turn which again changes the life circulation into a spiraling development - now the Sacrifice is demanded which we will less than ever before be willing and able to make... unless we, brought to the highest need, find ourselves suddenly prepared to pay the unknown Price: the giving up of everything for the sake of everything.

Thus this is the Going-around of "God's Angel" over the earth which confronts people everywhere with a situation that forces them to an actual confession to Yes or No, the Selection from On high, from which no man can withdraw. Here decency and goodness after human measure, religiousness or agnosticism, etc. etc. count for nothing because they are concerned *only* with the human soul actually confessing itself to Life or Death. It will *always* have to be a Jephta's Sacrifice because we will have to love Life more than the dearest form.

Only this preparedness will then function as the Lamb's blood on the door post, when the Angel goes by in the Night of the Holy Protection.

But this Attention and Involvement of GOD will at the same time be the manifestation of His Return: RETURN, not as mental Image, nor as Idyll, nor as a repetition of the well known.

Return as Novelty which contains everything past comprehensively in itself and establishes what was not-yet revealed in the human realm.

Return, not as satiation, sensation, or demonstration, but as Consummation which can be experienced only by the receptivity of the human soul longing for it.

Without receptivity for this, we experience *nothing*.

That sounds like it should speak for itself, but we are not even conscious that we lack precisely this receptivity. Grayness, emptiness, a lack, being deprived, being locked-out, the meaninglessness of our existence, of the occurrences around us, of the circumstances and occurrences in our lives, it is all a conclusion of lack of receptivity, projection of a lack of self-knowledge, which tries to justify itself in *judgment*.

For we may see and hear a lot, but these are only impressions of the senses. We are over stimulated and vulnerable and we call that "sensitive." But we *are* not sensitive.

Hearing and seeing in us have perished! As has perished the *exaltation of the soul* and thereby the use of everything else sanctified by it, which was given as *ability to experience*, as enlargement and elevation of the consciousness of life in the "transitions" that are now behind us, always as a Divine gift after a sacrifice in need, always as Response of Faith to faith, always as Arising from the dead.

That is exactly why we are the dead who bury themselves, because we have not, with inspiration and experience, dedicated to life everything that has thus been given to us, as living power and power to live. But it is dried up to a many sided mechanism, which functions autonomously. It has become a dead outfit, a dumb being-thus, which we thanklessly abuse. Abuse, because we do not dedicate it to the Service of GOD, but to the senseless hunt for satisfaction of a lesser caliber.

In us does not live the joy of movement as experience of being liberated from powerless rigidity which was removed exactly because the living being had stood its ground in that defenselessness in its erected Being. Our "ego" is a despot, even in its altruism! How little do we realize with our ego-loneliness that we are, in effect, liberated from the barren loneliness of before, because approaching and reaching each other has been given to us, observing and exchanging, feeling and understanding.

From what kind of life and death longing the senses must have grown! For it was concerned with experiencing and understanding, *not mechanical impressions.* The yearning to see is not a yearning for light reflexes, for the observing of images, but an inner desire to follow the course of the holy occurrences. The Indo-European root SEQ (see Latin sequor = I follow), from which our word to "see" is derived, proves this!

Thus, our hearing is not the result of the need to receive sound stimuli but to be able to *follow* the holy consummation. With tasting, it is not about tastiness but about a necessary choice between acceptable and not acceptable; and the sense of touch is not a dead detection of touching but the result of the longing for meeting, to experience identity.

Smell attracted Kore there where the God of the invisible world (Hades = Aides = the Unseen) took her to himself. And even if this story seems to our modern, Western dejectedness nothing but a friendly camouflage of an all too unlikely death, in truth it is an image of spiritual insight, the meaning of which had already been lost to the people of the classic era. In the antique era, however, people still realized that Divine Presence sometimes manifests itself to people by a Smell. This substantial Appearance is more a "precursor" than Hearing and Seeing. God chooses smell as the ethereal clothing and belonging to the moment. But people want to dictate God's Presence and choose smell and moment to make the "believers" undergo a pseudo-experience.

Language, developing only as the power to think took form, is the bridge given to us to overcome not only the loneliness of feeling with the voice, but with speech to overcome the pseudo-centrality of thinking, in the understanding of the relativity of emotional and mental images. A protection against otherwise inevitable monomania as a judgment over "forgetting" the only truly Central One.

But in us the eye has become a camera obscura and the ear a hearing aid. That is why Hearing and Seeing have perished in us; we have become the beings which Isaiah indicated: people who see but do not perceive, hear but do not understand.

The awareness of the only sanctifying use, the *experience* of the sense of the capabilities, has faded away. That goes for everything that thus has been given to man in the past after untold suffering, unspeakable living need, and has become his own.

The "ego" that is enclosed in its thinking realm as in a rampart that is a prison at the same time, resists its life task and the circumstances, and resists everything and everyone it meets with the measure of its mental images.

The delusion of norms, of objectivity, of equality and uniformity, of the impersonal, and consequently of rights and obligations flowing from those mental products, is the possession that rages everywhere, which is literally indomitable, and it promptly yelps, when, in the few moments of inner reflection, GOD'S will manifests itself, like Jesus at one time in the synagogue...

That is why we misunderstand the value of our life task, the value of our fate, for we stick to a fictitious image, to an image of how it would be "good," successful, happy, God-pleasing for everyone. Because of the spell of the thinking that values things only in norms, we forget not only our God-connectedness, but also our individual uniqueness. The denial of the personal, of individual truth, which is so typical of socialism and Marxist communism, is the fruit of the crass triumph of one-sided thinking that puts itself in the place of full human experience. Marxism is not awareness of reality, but a mental product. And so much are we all caught up in the usurpation of thinking that we do not understand this and collectively must suffer a long time for this and similar dictatorships of fictions, until we are healed from them.

For it all does not agree with us very much. The barrenness of the existence that we have implemented so stubbornly, has displaced all outer need to inner need. And the fact that suicide is by far more prevalent in the very countries where pseudo-love of mankind has imposed its system of pseudo-security and pseudo-safety in so-called social justice, has demonstrated *that idealistic government interference does not serve life but threatens it.* Equality is a trick of despotism. In a rigidly ordered regime the desperate youth rebels and we call that nihilism.

In the meantime this is not more than one facet of the evil that we perpetrate ourselves. With our withered individual lives goes a withered professional activity, the machine-like attention and dedication of energy to work that is not only not creative, but to which we can hardly dedicate heart and soul, despite all suggestion and pretense. With unequaled hypocrisy the reasoned, one-sided, half-mechanistic "distribution of labor" on the grounds of short term monetary advantage has been introduced, and the slowness of the soul of "labor" has let it happen. For injustice of this kind, for life-denial in general, such as it is being imposed by the powerful of the earth, a "counterpart" is necessary, which lets it happen to itself and consciously lets itself be abused for the sake of supposed safety and... carefree existence. Exploiter and exploited are the two faces of the same essence and the effect is always mutual. The *mental* relationship of employer-employee, to which human relationships are increasingly being reduced, is only a modern form of the age old desecration of life: Master and Slave.

No one *is* slave and no one has to become a slave, except *because of* his *unwillingness* to bring Jephtah's sacrifice! But this truth is harsh and who wants to listen? Who voluntarily resigns from a position of power? We'd rather suffer "manager's disease."

Incomparably more tenuous than the previous phases of expanding consciousness was the free development of the ego-consciousness which involved unheard-of temptation to degenerate into a goal in its own right. The "ego" and the collectivity of egos, which is a typical unreality, created a pseudo life and a pseudo life task, binding, forcing, enslaving, and putting human authority in the place of the one true Authority and the one true Power.

There is no escaping this except by rejecting the pseudo authority of this arrogance and to recognize only GOD's Authority, individually as well as collectively; not as a sacrifice to fictions and idols, but the Sacrifice of pseudo-autonomy. Not as a battle of human power against human power, but as abdication of ego-proliferation and we-proliferation, individually and collectively.

The liberation rests in, once again, motionlessly holding out, in, once again, being defenseless, in the bearing of solitude to be able to reach others. With the resurrection of our life consciousness the undefinable rapport between our physical body and its life source reconstitutes itself. It reconstitutes the true, purposeful, serving character of our entire organism. By fasting from emotional satisfaction in binding and exploiting, our emotional life, which had degenerated into a labyrinth of lust, is purified to bridging-intention from heart to heart, from person to person.

The liberation happens not in the least by humiliation of the "ego," by turning away from pseudo-centrality and its power back to the Almighty GOD, realizing and acknowledging powerlessness in a constant "Thy Will be done."

In that way, and that way alone, we take the first steps on the Rainbow-bridge from the devil to GOD.

In that way, and that way alone, our Receptiveness repairs itself and we will experience the Second Coming, not of Jesus, but of "God's Salvation," not of Christ as a rigid, dogmatic

Image, but of the Nameless One, GOD, whose manifested will people call Jesus Christ, because they always have to label things, even and especially what they neither know nor understand.

If we are prepared thus to confess our unreceptiveness to ourselves, our deafness and blindness, our denial of movement, our denial of the essence of Life and of our individual existence, then we will gradually let go of the systematic misjudgment of our life task, of what has or has not been apportioned to us. Then we will no longer go on with a forced struggle for possessions, power, honor and a categorical image of success, happiness, and life fulfillment.

Then we will - even if unaware - become receptive to the *unique* meaning of our life. We will realize that we have been confronted with an impenetrable Governance, which, for so long, did not appear to exist, because we drowned it out with the categorical misjudgment of the common standard-images concerning the value of everything and anything, with the aggressiveness of our Cradle.

Whether we are poor or rich, sick or healthy, prosperous or oppressed by bad luck,we will know ourselves face to face with the Mystery of Life. We will suspect a completely different why and wherefore than the meager conclusions of fragmentary, causal connections, which were bromides for so long.

For one and the same "fact" will prove to have an innumerable number of inner values as Why and Wherefore for different people, effective in God's Therapy.

The words, which we use as names, will prove to have a completely different meaning to the normal meaning. We will no longer be able to partake in the thoughtless discrimination between good and evil, favorable and unfavorable, and so on, all of it with no other validity than that of categorical misunderstanding. We will no longer be able to cry with the wolves in the forest because of one or another occurrence which is collectively misunderstood as a "calamity," much less thoughtlessly enjoy something that aims to realize the collective misunderstanding of a successful life.

Then we are prepared to postpone our conclusion about everything and anything, if possible, until the unique meaningfulness becomes clear to us. But with that we stand turned towards God, "listening" to what, we know inside, we will hear in due course... and understand.

And that is to be Shimeon, for Shimeon means "listening,"
and this *listening of the Soul* is the sanctification of
Hearing. It is once and for all the firm bottom (rock), on which
God's Saving Therapy founds the heavenly order, the true
order of life in us.

Of course we will painfully be Shimeon the Leper, that is the
"unclean listener," and that uncleanliness will lead to the well
known denial and betrayal, especially in confrontation with
pure accomplishment (Mark 14:1-11).

Who is that "Judas" whom we despise so much, who the
theologians and believers get rid of so easily by painting him
as a rebellious man, a thief and a traitor? Of whose name,
Jehudi Iskarioth, the theologians all this time cannot find the
meaning. For there is a town Kerioth but then why would Ish
not have been translated into Greek? The true nature, the
true role of this human figure in the manifestation of the
mystery of Life is so strange to us all, including the experts,
that we do not understand that it is us. We can not suffer the
thought, that we would be Judas, because we are Judas!
Jehuda, the Praised one. What mild humor! But then Iskarioth, what do we have to do with that? But sure! Nothing
characterizes us so much as the fact that we "are seized and
confused by the Spirit," that we promptly go into a panic at
the confrontation with the Manifestation of God's Will, that
we enter into unbearable tensions when God's Face turns to
us and enters our life! In Aramaic, Ithkerioth means: to be
seized, confused by the Spirit. Flattering it is not, but so much
the more undeniable for those who experience the Mystery as
mystery. Which one of us is *not* such a small one, seized, and
confused, who, "possessed" by fear of perishing, "hands over"
the Manifestation of God's Will to the power formation of
religious dogmatism and worldly violence?... to recognize,
precisely because of that, the reality, and to confess in forlorn-
ness and self-doubt: I have failed!

But the first step on the Way to Life has been taken. And the
one Necessity is not that we promptly receive Light on what
happens in us and to us, but that we realize that GOD's
attention is manifested therein.

And we will be moved by the depth of the apparently so
familiar human language. For every word has a deep meaning

through which the spiritual meaning of what happens can be indicated in veiled form and can be understood in due course. Thus every part of the body and every organ and every act become symbols of an abstract value. The physical life-processes reveal themselves as manifestations of cosmic occurrence. We really can not fail but in faithfulness to life, by denial of the arch qualities.

Thereby our failure becomes public in body and psyche. By that also healing becomes public, GOD manifests himself as the HEALER.

Our aroused receptiveness will make us pay attention to everything that is called force majeure and that truly turns out to be a Higher Power.

We can no longer observe a forced state of Rigidity, total or partial, of involuntary Immobility, of dysfunction of the organs, without realizing that we are face to face with a reminder of the first arch quality, without realizing that this is "so that GOD's Works may be revealed."

We can no longer meet the imposed immobility, the taking away of free Coming and Going, approaching and removing, doing and leaving alone, as a new immersion in the experience of inapproachability, without knowing the Mystery of GOD's Attention at work therein, for the sake of Life and for the sake of the human being who lives.

We can no longer see blindness and deafness, without believing in the heavenly involvement of the Seeing and Hearing of the soul therein.

We will no longer view a physical or mental "deformity" as if it were a defect to a machine or some electronic equipment nor regard heart disease as a defect to an engine.

We will no longer regard an occurrence of Fate as dumb coincidence, or misinterpret separation, loneliness, childlessness, suffering in sexuality, marriage or love, as pointless. But we will recognize the imposed want as a holy Fasting, as a preparation for something else, and the imposed loneliness we will understand more or less as a being emptied, the inaccessibility as a being preserved of the heart, which GOD has destined to be His Dwelling.

And everywhere we see Humiliation and immersion in Powerlessness, failure and ruin of human glory, there we will recognize preparation of re-establishment of the Remembrance and Surrender to the Almighty.

Only then will we lose the inclination to ask the loveless question: "Who has 'sinned,' this one or his parents?" (John. 9:2). For our attention no longer goes to "sin" and to "punishment." And likewise we do not get stuck in a mental explanation as with the debit and credit of "karma," for the Mystery does not reveal itself to intellectual positions and we expect insight in the heavenly guidance by revelation.

The human being in whom the unfathomable Contact with GOD has been reestablished no longer asks "why" but at most "what for?"

Our eyes are opened to these things only because we let our earthly "vision" be covered with the barren dirt which is put on our blind eyes by God's Salvation, God's Unfathomable Therapy; and in that accepted powerlessness "wash" ourselves in the streaming emotion which is sent (Shiloah).

Thus a person approaches more and more the Meeting with the Nameless one and the experience of His words: "See, I make all things new!"

For there is an immense parallelism between the way of Human development, the accomplishment by Jesus of Nazareth, the parousia or second coming as mass Mercy on humanity (in Hinduism: Vishnu-incarnation, in Buddhism: the Coming of the Lord of compassion, Maitreya), and the individual way of Salvation, Initiation, or Enlightenment.

In holding up in the threefold Temptation in Want and Loneliness, Jesus fulfilled the three Arch qualities of Life. In the passion, he absorbed the fallout of complete animality from the heart of mankind, and in his death, he founded, for all times, the possibility of sanctification of the person, elevation of the individual to eternal life, that is elevation from the "fall" of split consciousness and fulfillment of true Humanity here on earth.

Thus Jesus has in principle HEALED the Resistance of the human horde against the Authority of God.

His life, therefore, opened a new level of human life on earth, because he consummated the sanctification of the ego-consciousness in realization of the true relationship to GOD, synopsizing previous sacrifices of transition.

This also is a Jephta's Sacrifice, and it will be very difficult for the rare individual who makes it, as it was difficult for Jesus, but more so as he was the first one.

With his "Thy Will be done" and "In Thy Hands I commend my spirit" he irrevocably sacrificed the pseudo-autonomy of the "ego."

With the widening of his emotional life to all who "hear" him, he sacrificed individual hiding in personal sympathy and antipathy, with its consequential ties in a positive or negative sense.

With his continued "working" on the Task that had been given to him, he emptied his existence of all personal content that can be registered.

And by his defenseless suffering of a violent death, he sacrificed the satisfaction of physical experience in every sense.

Through that, and not because of idealistic-idyllic goodness and sweetness or any earthly heroism of defiance of life, his life forever remains a Token that is contradicted, and his appearance and disappearance had to become a Fall and Resurrection of many.

Between this timeless Message and us has been placed everything that human awareness could find as a defense and to render it harmless. In more aware peoples, the Romanization led to protests and rigidity in pedantry; the Slavic need for dreaming led to settling in emotional idylls. And as a final excuse, the fear of the inevitable that had come close reached for the Hellenic cult of thinking and beauty.

Rebirth set itself up against the Second Birth.

Apparently as a liberation from the Roman Catholic and later on Protestant crippling of life, the Renaissance and also Humanism (including today's variety) were a revolt against the recognized claims of the Inevitable Self.

Thank God that the depth of our being prevents us, in the long run, from staying in the non universally-unique. That is the chance for the Tidings, for it concerns not the unique in a race or people, but the universally and uniquely human which is elevated and elevates above that.

For somewhere we feel that we are involved. Somewhere we know ourselves related, we know ourselves to be included in the inevitability of all this.

We can do what we want or cannot do without but one day we will die anyway. And in this dying whatever we did not *give* freely is overpoweringly taken from us.

Only it is done to us in reverse sequence. We first die bodily and only after that does the ethereal body dissolve.

Our departure from time and space successively takes away all orientation, all proportions. The memory image that passes before our consciousness, and of which so many who turned halfway have testified, dissipates when it disappears from the sphere of orientation; it loses the coherence which it took from our relation with the objectivity of space and time. It is said: the dimensions seem to become impossibly big. That could be a reflex of our own going towards spacelessness.

Because of the same transition, also all our emotional attachments lose the ground that supports them. The pseudo-justification of our subjective emotional attitude must get lost completely in the process of vain revisions in ever growing spaciousness and ultimately dissolve into impersonal kindness.

Then the think-ego has nothing left that would perpetuate it, except for thinking itself, which, however, is turned into itself and cannot exist in the reality of the spiritual domain.

And in that man loses his mortal "self" in a total *powerlessness* in the face of the Truth of Almightiness.

"GOD is not a God of the dead, but of the living," Jesus says to the arrogant people who wanted to measure with the properties of the mortal world what Is in eternity (Mark 12:27).

Because all of this is so and will never change, that is why the Way, the Truth, and the Life can not be reduced to the risk free convenience of a mass, a psalm, and a sermon.

Nothing *has been* given but the *Following* of Jesus through Going of the Way that has been opened by him; following in suffering and need, want and ruin. Or, making do in open and hidden revolt and denial, only to experience at the time of death (despite all big talk) the Discovery of our Nakedness... and to return to GOD as one of the many who did not accomplish the unconscious Task.

Man's life-consciousness, developed to a fourfold quality, has led to the mental conclusion in spiritual circles that man has four mortal vehicles or bodies.

This is in the nature of thinking; we think no truth, but we form an image or projection of truth. Thus arises dogmatism, doctrines about the spiritual, that is the unknowable, unlearnable, which can only be *known* through revelation (not learned).

Man, in his fourfold consciousness, can not stop defining with his thinking what is spiritual and therefore not definable. This is psychologically understandable as a defense, an attempt to *maintain* oneself in the face of what is forever of higher value. There the "Uprising" commences.

Dogmatism is an attempt to master what overpowers us, by fixing it and organizing it. That is why Martin Buber says so rightly: "Das Dogma ist, auch wo sein Herkunftanspruch unbestritten bleibt, die erhabenste Form des Gefeitseins gegen die Offenbarung. Die will kein 'Perfektum' dulden, aber der Mensch mit den Künsten seines Sicherungswahns steift sie zur Perfektion ab.[3]" (*Zwiesprache* p. 37).

Dogmatic theorizing about Jesus of Nazareth therefore is not the work of "followers," but of scribes, people who hoped and believed that through knowledge orientation about Jesus, the right spiritual attitude (and probably also following) could be achieved.

Reflection, however, is always a form of stopping, and even distancing. Consciously or unconsciously, it is a symptom of "not-willing-yet" and leads to "never-going-at-all."

Thus, the painful arrogance of assertions about the humanity or divinity of Jesus has arisen, from people, who - whatever their orientation may have been - did not follow him, who did not participate in the revelation through suffering, death and resurrection, which alone leads to "knowing" and imparts the right to speak, because of changed BEING.

Not only did hatred and anger, strife and murder arise from that, but also all theories which acquired "authority" form serious obstacles for the adherents (and those who are influenced unconsciously) against following, against the revelation which would be theirs as a result.

---

[3] Dogma is, even when it has impeccable credentials, the most refined form of resistance to revelation. Revelation does not permit any past tense, but man with the art of his obsession for certainty makes it rigid to the point of perfection.

GOD manifests His Will in man when and how HE wants it. He does not obey human ideas and human reasoning. And it becomes really painful when dogmaticians contend that their doctrines were obtained through revelation. Revelation is revelation of truth, not formulations *about* truth. An outsider does not become an insider except by following and accomplishing.

That is exactly why theorizing is fatal, and leads to nothing but halting, skirmishes, and "treading water."

Knowledge, having this or that, is not where it is at, but a quality of Being. In the holy going towards this Being all Having is merely ballast.

Plutarch said: "Dying is initiation." In Greek that is a profound play on verbs from the same root, in which for dying, the euphemism "completing" is used and for initiation, a word that means perfection as well as purification and dedication.

But also here we discern an - ever so veiled - reference to the analogy indicated before. Initiation, salvation, liberation, illumination, finding peace, making immortal, entering the kingdom of heaven, the essence of the Process about which so much is said by those who have not even experienced the beginning of it, the essence of this Change is experiencing a loss of self for the mortal Four, so the immortal Three can be manifested.

Following Jesus is therefore a way of suffering, because it leads to Loss of self in the same sequence as Jesus suffered through it, and therefore in reverse sequence of what happens to a person during and after bodily death.

Now the world swarms with "experts." Not only the Grand Inquisitor has awarded himself the monopoly of Vicar of Christ, uncounted are those who have formed a power constellation, or at least a power center, be it on a smaller scale, also outside Christianity, for a similar assault on GOD's Power show up everywhere.

But Salvation or Liberation, the transubstantiation of the mortal Four is God's own Work and He does not let it be taken from His hands.

It is the heavenly attention for man which flows from God's Hand as the constancy on which Transformation happens, while the attention of man for God breaks the bane of matter and provides the basis for the transforming quality in matter.

When HE arranges it such that the bodily structure can be occupied by His Direction, then that relationship emerges, which after completed transformation has Inside-Life (eonic, eternal Life) for its measure of consciousness.

When death sets in, a general stimulus arises for the Four to fall apart, and thus inside-consciousness becomes free thereof. Whenever, through inside-consciousness, Involvement is manifested long before death, then the Four do not fall apart, then they become serviceable, supporting and helping, without impressing their own stamp on inside life.

It's no wonder that this requires long preparation, which relates very closely to what inside-consciousness will manifest through that particular person. This will *never* be possible without God's protection or there will be destruction: destruction, as it manifested itself in the few who came to some experience of inside at their own direction, and then wanted to let this maneuver in time and space.

Not only has a lot of "pseudo" been perpetrated, there has been a lot of freebootery by people, be it independent, be it in a relationship where a human being usurped the role of God (gurus and other initiators).

The parable of Jesus concerning the person who sat at the wedding dinner, but did not wear a wedding dress, is patently obvious.

When God directs His Attention in the human sphere, that Direction certainly enters this sphere, *but not as a human quality.* Therein lies the secret of Bridging such as HE can only accomplish. Whenever He directs this attention to a person, then that means that this person will be able to, or will be put in the position to, let this Bridging happen to himself.

How this consummation directs itself in the human sphere to human values is also a secret which can only be experienced by him in whom this comes to pass and in such a way that this person will be enabled to step on that Bridge for his own direction.

Of course, neither this person, nor another person can reduce *this* to a human concept.

The disowning of the "cradle" to which man lies chained is and remains God's Work. The inevitable demolition is deeper and more all encompassing than man with his unilluminated consciousness would ever be able to sanction and allow. The inadequacy of much that seems good and indispensable in human eyes, man himself can not fathom. On the other hand, he tends too much to self-rejection, where there is nothing reprehensible but that rejection, which is veiled arrogance and veiled resistance. Thus Salvation goes hand in hand with a lot of suffering, a lot of bitterness, and many skirmishes, which, in due course, will turn out to have been harmless and aimless.

We speak easily of Surrender, but when the moment asks for surrender, then we notice how difficult it is to us. Then we are shown up shamefully in that we never *give* ourselves but only *lend* ourselves to whom or what it may be. We lend ourselves to an adventure, to a tour de force. What is asked for is Surrender, and Surrender to... the Feared One at that.

When GOD penetrates the mortal structures of man in such a way that the owner can not get a bearing on that penetration but will have to receive what arises from that, that means precisely that His Will is done therein. And only this leads to elevation from split consciousness, the anchoring of consciousness in the awareness of the pairs of opposites of time and space, the bonds to our cradle.

Inside is not formed by stacking up of outside, as ponderousness and waving robes and cross and scepter, but is given to man at the blessed Second Birth; the Second Birth in which the consciousness is not transported into an improved version, but where a new consciousness arises from an unborn state.

What has been called cosmic consiousness, is *not* the completed mystical union, the Unification. It is the Overshadowing, momentarily, and therefore reflected and manifested in time as a memory image, as an "experience of Meeting," continuing in the existence in time and space.

So much has been written about Apprenticeship, or Initiation but the reality does not let itself be captured in a description.

It is certain that no man is an Initiate except when he is not aware of it in any respect, and, on the contrary, feels more than ever removed from any well founded initiation whatsoever.

An Initiate always has the skirmishes of the "possessed" against him sideways. Sideways, because the despicableness of the possessed contrasts too sharply with the difficult progress of the Initiate, right through the middle of the possessed.

Initiate is to be well known, and therefore unacceptable for the masses.

Initiate is to give God's Faithfulness to the masses.

Initiate is to know GOD where it seems impossible to accept Him. To understand Him above one's own understanding.

Initiate is to throw oneself to Him, notwithstanding Him.

"Technically" the Transformation is consummated in a Surrender of the "ego," the dethronement of thinking and the experience of powerlessness, through an emptying out of the heart and everything to which it had become attached, and emptying out of that registration of our experiences, which we call life-content, to a transubstantiation of the physical body.

Only when this preparation is complete, does the pouring out of Light, the positive Penetration, the Entering through the gates of heaven, the highest experience of Love, through which the walls that enclose consciousness fall away and Unity happens and continue to happen.

Everything that man had gathered in vessels with balm and oil, taken from the earth, GOD lets it flow back to what is the earth's.

No calculation will ever figure out what it has cost in tears and human suffering. But it will flow back to those earthly paths, where it will dissolve in the rivers of despair and disgrace and form a balm for the wounds which the Father makes.

Consolation is nothing, despair even less.

But to let the heart fall in these rivers is the only ransom which the Father and His son will give.

* *

We are now experiencing a fullness of time, the end of one period and the transition to a new Era.

In time past, man has proven to be completely incapable of populating the earth and to give the earth what is its due in conjunction with the forces of nature.

Therefore, a Milestone will have to be placed somewhere in the world as a *confirmation* of what so many have confessed to as the only necessity for this world.

For that confirmation GOD directs Himself to a called one with a specimen, an Assignment, through which the elevated line of the "Davids" regenerates as a Specimen of Times and makes "Israel" appear where it is necessary, to squash the repulsive time scruples.

Thus the Golden Thread is brought into the pattern and woven through, however much this pattern is permeated with the repulsiveness of the conditions. Exactly because of that, the Golden Thread will show up the pattern as "played out."

Our society *is* no society. Many things do not tolerate each other in the combinations of social structures and, if necessary, the most well intended negations are possible if it concerns the maintenance of the entire social structure.

If it is a cage, in which primitives, half primitives, and innocents are locked up together, still we would rather bear this than to open the door and let everyone go his own individual way. Freedom and equality are discussed, but we work with force, individually and collectively. Nowadays this circle is drawn wider and we want to reduce everything to a social structure, to arrive in this manner at the dream image that is really the object of our pursuit: the ROBOT, which then - waiting for the latest inventions - also will acquire "eternal life" on earth.

This is the pinnacle of absurdity, the total denial of Life, and the three arch qualities at the same time.

Against that, GOD puts the Living Man, who is conscious of his Task on this field of death.

For the Response of GOD to this composite denial of life is not "destruction" but Selection, that is to say pressure to respond to His Offering.

Response as a Yes or a No.

Therein the Selection happens, in that people in their judgment about what is offered select their own judgment about themselves, *avow* themselves as "usable" in God's Plan for the New Era or "unusable" and therefore superfluous and destined to disappear.

This is how it has always gone and this is how it will go this time.

The general Adversity is the Crisis which is the "judgment" and the separation in this Transition. The general Adversity itself is the means in God's Hand to make humanity, in its divisiveness, experience one and the same undeniable experience of POWERLESSNESS which will bring leaders and their followers to deep discouragement.

Thus, human-kind which either denied GOD's ALMIGHTINESS officially or negated it in practice, is REMINDED of the fundamental truth which it would have had to abide by as a quality of life: its relationship to GOD.

The presence of, at least, one human being in whom this relationship has blossomed to a streaming celebration of The Way, The Truth, and The Life, will, in every appearance, rekindle the CONSCIENCE that has been buried under compromises or replaced by theologically or ideologically trained behavior.

No mere attitudes will be able to stand up in the confrontation with the Reality that is revealed overwhelmingly. But depression and need of old are the best ground for new hope.

For not in time but in the attitude of the soul The Kingdom is or is not "near." And nothing can be so consoling, hope inspiring, and animating as the experience of the reality of Life and the freedom that is no attitude, but a real way of Being.

Nearly all people are educated in the bane of arid moralistic decency, founded on some sort of dogmatism.

For all of us our Conscience has, through wrong information since our early childhood, become the voice of a deeply hidden, short-changed father figure which reminds us of our guilt. This pseudo conscience already is trained behavior which can be further subdivided into Jesuit-conscience, Calvinist-conscience, fascist-conscience, communist-conscience, etc., and let's not forget democratic-conscience.

This pseudo-conscience is the co-determinant of the sad orientation in normal existence and its life-denying regime, its low striving for success, its wretched obligations to fulfill the mold of an upper, middle or lower-class existence with its neurotic "Geltungswille"[4] and its neurotic pseudo society. A pseudo society, led by pseudo shepherds, who lead the herd to the slaughter house with nice stories, one to suit every taste.

And as individuals oppose each other in hardly controlled, neurotic aggressiveness, thus nations, represented by simi-

---

[4] Urge to manifest oneself.

larly neurotic people, face-off evidently not as brothers, not as free entities, each with its own respectable calling, but as patients, as total or semi-madmen, who will not shun any lowly deed to realize their delusions at the expense of one or more others... with a pseudo-conscience of their own making.

That *can* not be cured and saved from destruction with more concentrated preaching of moralistic guidelines, not even by proffering holy scriptures.

That can only be healed by salvation from the sad isolation from the one source of life, by repairing the awareness - however weak - of connection and inclusion in one cosmic, living, and imperishable Connection!

Recovery of *the inner knowledge* that man is not just a foundling cut loose from the womb, a floating island of life on the heartless, senseless sea of dead and living forces in which, at most, he finds some consolation by connection with another being that has been similarly duped, with whom he then commences the self-preservation duet called a family.

Rekindling of the living *awareness* that man exists in eternal connection with the background of an unknown past, a misunderstood purposefulness in the present, and an unknowable destination, staying here on earth in a meaningful life task, which can not be analyzed and comprehended by his mind, but with which he is called in a silent dialogue to fulfill a *mission* which - however little it can be defined in precise detail - essentially must be a manifestation of faithfulness to Life,precisely because it is a life-task.

This awareness works as an enormous liberation: liberation from the troubles caused by the impossible fulfillment of the "rights and duties" of living by the mold, waning of the compelling, intruding impressiveness of the leading principles which were misunderstood as categorical-absolute, respect for the categorically misunderstood individual life-tasks.

For categorical valuations are *all* wrong and fatal in their complete denial of what is unique. A person who suffers poverty *is* not a person who - oh, what a pity! - can not buy this or can not do that which the rich neighbors from across the street can all do. But it is a person whose life task will be fulfilled and manifested sooner and purer, exactly because of *that* life-condition. And the way it is here, that is how it is with *everything*, not *one* thing excepted, in spite of all appearances to the contrary. What a breath of fresh air, what a feeling of liberation, not to feel handicapped by no money or no car or no television, or no power and no glory, no good eyes or no good ears, or whatever "shortcoming" or whatever "defect!" What a deep Turning in the orientation towards fulfillment of life, what a totally different division of the *attention* and dedication of life energy to the unique, individual life task! And now one can be inclined to strive for an idyllic image of a Good Lord based on prejudices from one's upbringing or of one's own making or be equally prejudiced in not accepting this "Father-image" in one's life vision *which can impossibly be a priori "vision"* but even the deferred judgment, even only the negative *relinquishing* of the delusions that were drilled into us, of self-determination and being-left-to-one's-own-devices with all its consequences, leads a person into an impersonal but real knowledge of a connection with the fathomless depth, above which his personal, manifest, human existence is like a leaf on a huge tree atop the invisible life-root.

Naive and cerebral is the question yes-God/no-God, as if reflection (in which the fear of meeting is already manifest!) would reveal what life would keep from us as experience. But even if the fear of life drives us to flight into judgmental pro and con, the confrontation with realized Life works right through the armor plating of self-denial and does its Healing work.

For that is exactly why the appearance of a truly living person not only upsets people but this makes them throw-up their ego-structure like dice before the Cross.

Thus this first rekindling of the conscience of the soul is the first Manifestation of God's Interference which prevents destruction.

Yes, He uses a person for that. He manifests his Will, His Bridging Intent in the accomplished Bridging in a human child. How much is human or divine in such a person, does not concern the lookers-on, but especially that we will want to assert deterministically, time and time again.

These manifestations have occurred every time when the degeneration of humanity made it necessary. Never the same as a dumb repetition. God does not repeat himself. But history registered it, in whatever way, and mentions the appearance of a Savior, a Saoshyant, an Enlightened One, a Liberator, a Krishna.

It would be a miracle if the startled group that experienced it would not promptly want to make such an appearance into its property, its monopoly, and would testify of him in that spirit of misrepresentation.

Man is like that.

These appearances are rare but they are necessary. Not the *person* in question returns from time to time, but the Spirit of GOD manifests itself again in a human being as a First Bridge.

The blessed influence, which will then arise, when GOD connects himself with a person in this manner, does not live or die with the fatal incantation to which the person has aroused himself, but in itself gives Salvation in a widely branched way, which no human being can oversee.

The direct Involvement that is now happening thus opens the possibility for a new kind of humanity: human existence on a higher level of life, directed at the connection from man to man, realized more deeply than in nature alone; revealing the connection of soul in the fields of soul - not of man and man but - from *man and his own integral connection with higher levels of consciousness.*

The Manifestation in a person causes the Word to resound anew; to be given anew what has not been asked for, what wants to be kept to be toppled, what was declared "holy" to be destroyed, and what distress and pressure have made into unanimous defense in the stream of chaotic Word-breach to be switched off.

A person who serves like that has the Authority of the Word and the power to equalize every infraction of the laws of creation. Thus arises the awareness: "See he has made all things good," but also the dogmatic, erroneous conclusion: Forgiveness of "sins."

Recovery of the fundamental awareness of connectedness to God, awareness of the lifelong enjoyment of God's Attention, means repair of the barren "rapport" with the sphere through which life energy flows towards us. Through that the "double" revives from its dried out condition. The condition of awareness of connection, the recognition of not being cut-off in a loneliness that proves autonomy but rather being protected in the dependence of what is Causal and Overpowering, gives the individual life back to Him who gave it.

Exactly because life is dedicated to God, it remains at His Disposal. Thus, our eyes are opened for the timeless meaning of the biblical "being dedicated to the Lord." When God's Angel, going around in the night of the times, takes away these and "passes by" (Pasach!) those, then that is because the latter *had already been given back to GOD!* That is the background of the age-old ritual which still resounds in the Gospel according to Luke 2:22, where the Jesus child was "introduced" to GOD, or better: dedicated, *offered up.* The Hebrew word gives the key.

It was customary to lay the living form back in God's Hands, whence it had been received, *and that is why the life that had been entrusted was preserved.* Rededication to GOD means truly: Thy Will be done, in Thy Hands I commend my spirit. The reconstituted relationship brings healing from sickness and need.

That is why the rekindling of the conscience of the soul is *the Turning,* which the oppressed person lets the Caller consummate in himself. The life that has been reoffered to God is "preserved."

It is the solid rock on which can be built and will be built that which is resistant against rains and storms. Just as the newly-born in Israel were offered up to the Life-giver by the God-dedicated mother, many will need one who has been called to that task as a mother image which "carries" them in a trust-inspiring way, in their feeling of inner impotence and feeling-lost to the realization: receiving God's helping and uplifting Attention in their need.

For continued attention given to the Elevated One, in lacking almost everything that satisfies human existence, in being passed up for everything that could quiet the longing of the heart, creates not only *space* in a person, into which God can go; but the waiting sanctifies by relinquishing *time.* Also this is necessary.

Streaming consciousness of the Connection can not be stopped by anything or anyone, but will gradually fill those places which have become empty by rejecting time. Because of that, a lot can be set free that, in truth, is Experience, simple, direct Exchange between God and the consciousness of the person. "Blessed are those who do not 'see' but still believe."

Thus a person is prepared for the fulfillment of a Mission, a mission which is not an imposed task, accomplished resentfully, but an occupation which flows from the state of Being that has gradually been accomplished.

Thus a person becomes Guardian, no longer as one who "waits" in lacking, but one who Guards especially those who are waiting, who as "prodigal sons" anew put themselves in His Hand, and who now have to wait in trust for how His Attention works in them, helping and uplifting. And one waits three days, but another waits thirty years, before the emptiness in space and the emptiness in time give him back the Receptiveness with which he can experience the given Attention with his attention, and with that knows his life to be led to an incomparably higher level.

Then he will also "hear" the Word of God in recognition when it once again addresses its soundless sound to people in a human voice and in human words.

This is only possible when the Great Bridging towards the conscious inside-consciousness has happened in one who was touched in his center. When, in a person, the rule of the Four has made room for the free manifestation of the Three, all destructive working of the instinct is forever exorcised. A person like that receives from the Father the authority of the Son, the power to speak His Word and to do His Work. That is: to do as he "sees" the Father do (Greek: krisin poiein!) and to speak as he "hears." Out of his own volition such a person will not do anything ... because he can't. The person who is transformed by the Holy Spitit, died and reborn, is, like God's Spirit itself, unfathomable in his justice. "No one" knows from where he came nor whither he goes. He comes and goes as he is sent, for he comes and goes in The Open Field.

The Word of God is eternal, therefore unique, not repeatable. Unauthorized repetition of the form in which it once sounded, is misuse of the Word. The Word is momentary; God lets it dissipate where the need calls and He takes pity. To "hear" the Word, the preparatory "bottom formation" is necessary, the arousal of receptiveness.

The Working of the Word is "life giving" (Greek: zoopoioon, life-making, living-making - John 5:19-21). The human word reaches people through their natural hearing and works as values which are determined by the judging mind.

God's Word, on the contrary, does not get trapped in the cumbersomeness of senses and brain. It works directly in the Chakras and thence in the endocrine glands. That is why no man can speak God's Word, unless Aaron's Staff is in full blossom in him, the water has been turned into wine, the lights have been exchanged, the Holy Lake has been crossed and the continuity has been bred which shows day and night as the streaming celebration of The Way, The Truth, and The Life.

An individual Transformation like that is rare, but it is necessary as a preliminary accomplishment for the opening of an elevation of the level of life by a transformation which is impersonal and gradually working for many.

Once again there is religious (and agnostic!) expectation everywhere, of what is known intuitively as Coming; everywhere we expect: *that which will make everything good.*

God's blessed Interference is expected but the formulations of the expectations are so judgmental that they do not recognize each other and sometimes not even themselves as an expectation of this condition!

Human expectations are congelations in which people are trapped in expectation of...?

No time or space can however congeal God's liberating Manifestation.

God's Word is also His Deed.

And His Deed is also our Salvation.

And the expectation of the Messiah is His Belief in *us*, who rejected what He offered, and still reject what He offers.

GOD *is* no expectation!

He is the slow Fulfiller of everything that the expectation could not even accept *as* fulfillment.

In that He is the Only One who arouses the Relationship which excludes all expectation and which binds and realizes for all time.

As little as before, also this time will His interfering Manifestation be acceptable to the images that have been formed of it, and which people try to superimpose on reality.

The illusion of autonomy and pedantry, of power-cult and man-worship that proliferates today is certainly no less enchanting and blinding than the rigid barrenness which Jesus broke through.

The Uprising of the Masses was *released* by his fruit-bearing accomplishment but will now be *uprooted* permanently. Where better could this start than where Jesus ended?

The arrogant display of human power and human authority will liquidate itself in powerlessness and bewilderment. And the general Distress that arises in that way is turned to "good" by GOD. Destruction will happen on a large scale in various places on earth to make room for what will come, but not in the form of a world war.

The uncounted and their leaders, who have pursued *power* and the enforcement of their delusions, will be brought into a position of total *powerlessness* by force majeure and will be brought to perplexity through being overpowered by unsolvable problems.

Liberation will not come as the glory of the most infernal weapon of destruction, as the triumph of Cain-tactics, but we will be liberated from exactly that by being placed in the defenselessness of Abel.

The Word will sound with a directness that needs no explanation, as an unmasking of one delusion after another, light giving, hope giving, arousing expectation and accomplishing the turning towards the Goal that God will give.

It will arouse feelings of guilt in the sectors where this is needed, in order to be able to give Medicine, calming and vision giving, to dissolve chaos into a more conscious relationship with life.

The walls, which have surrounded and covered up the Word that Jesus spoke, will give way and be destroyed.

People have confined themselves to love, like a sort of mutually serving emotion, which finds its place in the world daily in unending variation. God will give manifestation of Love without the equal of human procrastination and human cleverness. Conclusive Love will manifest itself in everything as beginning and end in one, where distress, death, and depression can no longer be borne in the human sense.

God Himself comes to creativity in the formless beginning and absoluteness of what Is, in Him, through Him for the original laying of the first stone for the New Building, dedicated to man.

The New Time brings a new measure of human relationships which will be built on the foundation of brotherhood.

Thus, human existence on earth will be healed to a state of fundamental health, to a higher level of life-realization, because the inbred connection with God will manifest itself more and more in the attitude and the work of people. Gradually through that, the law of the Four will no longer be automatically authoritative and what happens will no longer be entirely obscured into an experience and registration of categorically misinterpreted form-meanings.

Gradually the constant Dialogue, the continual exchange between God and man will be accessible and be accessed. Then man will no longer be a self repeating puppet on a string in the cradle-game, but he will be able to totally dedicate himself to the unique accomplishment to which he has been called, in harmony with his being.

Just as in the individual Liberation during existence on earth, this general Interference will not manifest its fourfold Workings in a dumb sequence of four subsequent accomplishments.

Nonetheless, the same direction can be recognized as in the process of Jesus' accomplishment, as much in the process of Initiation as in the renewed Outpouring of Blessing, which is often called the Second Coming.

The same applies in the response of people.

The ever stronger striving for increased material well-being, the rapidly developing medical care and materialistic medicine, the preoccupation with youth, sports and self-aggrandizing socialism and communism, are all unconscious responses to God's Attention which is aimed at uplifting life, misunderstood in a one-sided attitude, through professional, social or individual-psychological *misunderstanding*.

All these involvements sprout from the emotionally laden *mental sphere*. Typical of these are depth-psychology and psychiatry-turned-philosophy.

The equalization which is apparent in all these involvements, is like the finger print of the originator, because the *robot* stems from the analytic-deterministic thinking, from the mental sphere of consciousness, not from the emotional sphere, not from the ethereal sphere, or from the material sphere. Recognizing the origin is the start of the unmasking, the discovery of the driving *motive* of all this striving. Particularly, this motive is of course *unconscious* and covered over by a label of love for mankind and love of life! The motive that lies behind that is less "lovely," it is aversion to suffering, aversion to disease, aversion to distress and aversion to want. Aversion which found its pseudo justification *NOT in reality but in cerebral misinterpretation of reality.* The tragedy of suffering is in the misunderstanding of it, in the misunderstanding of mental shortsightedness. The tragedy is in the delusion of pointlessness, needlessness, and ineffectiveness. There lies the root of the aversion and revolt, which in their ignoble heroism pride themselves and adorn themselves with qualities which are supposed to give their success an aura of welldeservedness.

No, Life does not triumph like that but *disguised death* triumphs like that. In all "ordering," all so-called organization, the cold interference shows, the manipulation, the machine, which tries to put itself in the place of the one life-power-source: the Heart.

Thus thinking usurps the life sphere and tyrannizes the sphere of feeling and the material sphere. In the emotional sphere, the delusion of equality gives powerful support to hidden jealousy.

For the poison beaker of thinking does not confine its intoxication to the over-accentuation of the self-centrality and its accumulation to a many-headed, seemingly unanimous *we!* The poisonous preoccupation denies the unique everywhere, in all areas of awareness and brings the multitude in to a desecration and violation of consciousness in those spheres.

In the emotional sphere this causes not only excessiveness, to which man tended of old in this sphere, but replaces this "prostrating himself" with a pseudo-saturation in watching and listening to the real (or unreal) emotional experiences of *others.* Literature, drama, film, records, tapes, radio and television massively seduce us to "vicarious experience," just like sports games and races massively seduce us to "vicarious movement." The dogma of "vicarious suffering" acquired respectable company! This has nothing to do with moralistic scruples but with awareness of life-desecration, and it does not deny other value.

In the ethereal sphere, it is the self-centeredness which has induced individual and group-wise rebellious bondage to religious and non-religious spiritism. This is no less an addiction than that to alcohol or morphine. It misdirects the spiritual attention (just like narcotics and pursuit of sensations) away from the holy meaning of the individual life. It does not respect the separation made by GOD and acquires pseudo-satisfaction from sickly receptiveness, from what appear to be utterances of beloved relatives or respectable strangers, but in truth are echoes, which systematically correspond to the emotional condition of those who are oriented this way, *and turned away from life.*

Of the same order is the preaching by those who were not called, not only those strangely-overcome individuals who, at inconvenient places and moments, direct the sultry stream of their words at the surprised and unwilling, but the countless "priests" trained and initiated by people who misuse the Word to discharge their own misunderstood tensions and especially those who know how to fascinate thousands and tens of thousands in mass-preachings with what purports to be conversion of souls but in truth is ethereal dispersal of seed, ejaculation.

In the material sphere a body cult arose which only partly improved the bodily condition. For at the same time the excesses manifested themselves, in the desire for records, the isolation of body-cult as a goal in itself. The naive fall of man in binges and one-sided body-care which is from a time long gone, has been changed into the misuse of the body as if it were a machine; getting the maximum out of it for a lesser goal; to deny it and short change it in its rhythms and simultaneously to worry about sickness and death; and thus the administering of a thousand medicines from tonics to tanning clinics and "the five vitamins that you lack every day." That is the pseudo conscience, which does not think of stopping this or any other shortfall, but stupidly tries to compensate. The truly despicable drive for compensation comes over us at the sight of anything that disturbs us. It is a systematic attempt to "buy out" of *addressing* what has been given, to remove anything that could be disturbing for a continued experience of comfort, a continued freedom of tension, a restful lying in state in a self-willed Death!

Thus we have prepared ourselves a fourfold grave as never before, and an unequaled need awaits us, to be awakened from the grave and to arise as a true human being, as a Son of man.

For this Arousal will not only lead to a higher level of life, but it opens in that and through that - even if only a few will want to go the required road of suffering - *the awakening consciousness of immortality* because the purified mental sphere no longer blocks and covers up the access to the thinking of the soul. This, then, in its consummation is the beginning of the experience of Love which is immortal, a manifestation of Eternal Life.

Strong and unmovable is the hand of the Carpenter's son who has loosened the rusted screws of evil and has worked on the dried out wood until roses sprouted from it.

The gardener's son uproots thistles and thorns, and cuts the wild sprouts. And in the soil that was well prepared by his Father, he sows the seed of Light, from which New Life will soon bloom.

*   *
*

*

* *

For see: it is not at all about "sins" of man and about "punishment" which one could suffer with repression of inbred urges and with imposed virtuousness. It is not about "forgiveness of sins" either, nor about the "Lamb of God" which would have been "sacrificed" for our sakes!

All this is the ignoble delusion of the fools who cuddle up to the deceptive images of times long gone and who have kept the countless in the bane of fear and a feeling of dependence with their pseudo authority.

But it *is* about the cancellation of the "hamartia," that is the failing of the world. (*die Fehle der Welt, as Luther translated it*)

It is not about a Lamb (Hebrew: Taleh) of God but about a true servant of God (Aramaic: Taljah), a person who is willing to suffer this "failing" to the end in God's liberating Therapy and thus to open the access to a higher level of human life.

Theological speculation does not lead to clarity in that, but what has been cited above from the Book of Nature makes us understand that now is upon us the reduction of human authority in all its aspects to the modest proportions which correspond to its condition;

that now the pseudo centrality on which this authority is founded will have to make way for the Authority of the One Central One;

and that against this Intercession of the Almighty the opposing arrogance of human, worldly, and spiritual authority in all its sections will prove powerless.

Only who is prepared to sacrifice not only his presumed authority but also his entire humanity without reserve for this Manifestation of God's Will, will in this holy Process be the Servant destined for that by God Himself, who will be a blessing for mankind.

* *
*

Invitation to
Het Oude Loo

In the ancient castle "Het Oude Loo" at Apeldoorn (Holland) from time to time Meetings are held[1] of about one hundred people of diverse outlooks, positions, professions, nationalities, and races, invited to reflect and speak during three days on peace-making by orientation towards the sole maxim:

GOD FOUNDER OF THE WORLD AND THEREFORE INVINCIBLE

The initiative hereto was taken in the spring of 1951 by a few Dutch people who realized that the crisis through which mankind is going now, is greatly due to the fact that for a long time and on a large scale Man's actual conduct has gravely ignored the truth that Man does not rule the world, but the Founder of this Universe governs His creation. Consequently the world-peace can hardly be promoted more direct and more effectively but by reorientation towards said fundamental truth.

At these Meetings some prominent people from various countries at the request of the organizers submit their individual views on the world situation and the promotion of peace, thus expressing their prominence in the form of an address. By prominence is meant: men's activity in the world as guides, leaders or shepherds of men in whatever sphere of life.

"Het Oude Loo" aims at being an Open Field amid all the groups and institutions; and Open Field where men meet without dominating, where men testify without making propaganda.

The unrestricted space of this Open Field is not the private property of anyone, but offers to everyone an opportunity to revise his individual outlook under the sole truth already mentioned.

Endeavouring to approach God from this starting point, without any label, without any dogma, without any structure of doctrinal speculation, is the sole justification of the organizers before God and the world.

It is not for the organizers to judge any religious institution or movement, but it is their task in this world of hardened

---

[1] The meetings were held from 1951 - 1968, for details see the introduction.

materialistic moulding and equally rigid doctrines to offer an Open Field for reorientation in the individual lives of men towards their Sonship to God.

The organizers feel convinced that incorporation into some form of organization would inevitably result in adding one figure of power to the countless figures of power already existing, which although initially meant as a means to an end, always gradually become an end in themselves, absorbing the love, the devotion and the energy which are due to the Unseen and His Plan. Therefore they will not create any organization and in general invite people to one Meeting only, because they will not tie anyone. The organizers simply act as preparers and as guards for the respectation of the aim during the Meetings. Thus abstaining from organizing and managing they thrust to leave the greatest possible space for Divine Guidance.

The addresses are not exemplary but merely serve as instigations to the free exchange of views that follows. All guests are expected not to consider themselves as mere members of the audience, but to take an active share in the work, either in individual conversation or in talks of small groups such as are formed unintentionally. The formation of large groups should be avoided, because this tends to reduce the activity to just a few, the rest being mere listeners.

For the same reason improvisations are avoided, though the organizers may request someone to give an expose in exceptional cases.

In this way the Meetings are prevented to serve merely for the confirmation and strengthening of views and convictions already existing with the restrictions inherent thereto, whereas now there is a maximal chance for spontaneous recognition and acceptance of such fragments of truth as proffered in other people's utterances, instead of fostering selfsufficiency and propagating preconceived notions.

You can order copies of this book, or put your name on the list for announcements of new titles.

JWK Publications
40 Rampart Road
South Norwalk, Ct 06854-2417

When ordered from us, the price of this book is $13.95, postpaid in the continental US. Sales tax additional for Connecticut residents.
Make checks payable to **JWK Publications**.